Presented to:

Date:

From:

Volume 4
*Navigating
Life's
Storms*

Daily
Strength
for the
Battle©

You,
God's Word,
5 minutes

By Scott & Judy McChrystal

Daily Strength for the Battle:
Navigating Life's Storms
By Scott & Judy McChrystal

Published by Warrior Spirit Publications.

Contact information:
Web site: *www.dailystrengthforthebattle.com*
E-mail: *contact@dailystrengthforthebattle.com*
Mail: *Warrior Spirit Publications*
      P.O. Box 8125, Springfield, MO 65801

Design by Marc McBride

ISBN: 978-0-98481-190-8
Printed in the United States of America.

This devotional is dedicated to the courageous men, women, and families of our military community. They understand that living on planet earth poses many hardships and challenges, yet they bravely navigate through life's tight places. Their sacrifices on a daily basis enable our nation, under God, to remain as the "land of the free and the home of the brave."

Contents

Negative Impacts

Positive Impacts

Contents

Warriors Have Needs

Choices

Future Possibilities

Scott McChrystal's Strength for the Battle is a compact and inspiring volume. It connects the precious promises and truths of God's Word with the real world. This is straightforward talk from a soldier who has been in the heat of battle. But it is also the heart of a chaplain's message: encouragement and empowerment from God's unfailing love in Jesus Christ.

— Chaplain (Major General) Kermit D. Johnson, USA (Ret.)

Chaplain Scott McChrystal is a combat veteran and Spiritual Warrior who has captured the essence of winning the daily fight against mankind's' spiritual enemy. This is a good field manual for every Christian who wants to be prepared for battle.

— LTG Jerry Boykin, USA (Ret.), former Commander of Delta Force and Commander of USASOC

Chaplain Scott McChrystal served as one of the most beloved chaplains ever at the U.S. Military Academy at West Point. Standing behind Chaplain McChrystal is a plethora of experiences in touching the lives of thousands of America's magnificent warriors. My personal experience with Chaplain McChrystal at West Point and during other opportunities verifies my confidence, for I have seen the excellence of his ministry in operation.

— Rev. Dave Roever, Decorated Vietnam veteran; military speaker

Every man, particularly a warrior, needs time every day with his King. Focused, purposeful, gripping time. And if he's a busy man (know any warrior who's not?), the punch of that time is served well by a directed devotional book like this one offered by my friend, Scott McChrystal, who is himself a tested warrior. And a busy, focused, and purposeful man. Enjoy the journey with him. Drive on!

— Stu Weber, former Special Forces Officer and
Vietnam veteran, author, international speaker,
Pastor of Good Shepherd Church in Boring, Oregon

Introduction

> *Praise be to the God and Father of our Lord Jesus Christ, the Father of compassion and the God of all comfort, who comforts us in all our troubles, so that we can comfort those in any trouble with the comfort we ourselves have received from God.*
> *(2 Corinthians 1:3–4)*

Do you find that life today seems to have more trouble and difficulties than just a few years ago? I do, and I don't believe it's my imagination. Even as I write this introduction, I have family and friends who are trying to navigate through some kind of a storm. I imagine you can say the same.

These storms are impacting us in ways that are not always easy to spot, at least initially. Increasingly, people across our country are manifesting signs that stress has invaded their lives in harmful ways. This stress is not so much in response to physical threats like that produced by hurricanes, tornadoes, or flooding.

Contemporary stress results more from psychological threats stemming from a rapidly changing culture. These stressors tend be more pervasive, persistent and difficult to recognize. For example, think about the area of communications. Cell phones and computers have boosted our ability to stay in touch, but consider the down side. We all know people, maybe family members, whose lives have been hijacked by various addictions: video games, pornography, gambling, and even social media. And it's not slowing down.

Since 9/11, the military community has experienced stress on steroids. In addition to the contemporary threats mentioned above, we've had a protracted war to fight, war that has demanded far more from the military than any segment of our society. In a negative sense, our warriors and families have been "double dipping" from the ocean of stressors that are part of life in the 21st century.

The number one stressor by far is work, but several others contribute significantly to challenges we are experiencing: increased crime and violence, social isolation and loneliness, negative peer pressure, declining morals, and eroding family and religious values. And of course, economic problems are on everyone's minds these days. Finally, the pace of life for most is just plain hectic, if not frantic.

You don't need me to tell you about more problems or to convince you that stress is picking up speed. You want answers and solutions. You want to know that there is hope, and that the future is not all darkness and gloom. And as the title of this devotional book suggests, you want to know that there is a way to navigate through the storms of your life.

BLUF (Bottom line up front): Yes! There are answers and solutions. There is hope. You do have a future — a good one. And the best news of all is that God is for you, not against you. Not only can He help you navigate through your storms, but He will also go with you and even guide your ship if you will let Him.

But you must choose. God will not force you.

Participation in the storms of this life is not optional. But some seem to navigate through them with less damage and more resiliency.

In His teaching, Jesus never shied from the hard truth. Shortly before His crucifixion, He spoke to His disciples: "I have told you these things, so that in me you may have peace. In this world you will have trouble. But take heart! I have overcome the world" (John 16:33).

Notice in this verse that Jesus tells His disciples that this world is full of trouble. The word trouble comes from the Greek word *thlipsis*. The word carries with it the idea of being crushed, squeezed, hemmed in, or put under great pressure.

Jesus can help you. And He will help, but it's not automatic. We must decide to believe, trust, and obey.

A good starting point comes when we realize that the Christian life is not without storms. Problems, troubles, and stress don't disappear when we decide to follow Jesus. I never cease to be amazed at the misconceptions that many people, even Christians, have about what Christian living is supposed to look like. Below are three of the commonly held mistaken beliefs about Christianity:

- *Christians should not have any problems.* From Genesis to Revelation, the Bible is consistent:

Mankind has problems. The New Testament writers, particularly those who wrote letters, spent much of their time addressing problems. Time and again they warned fellow Christians not to be surprised at the troubles they would face. Jesus had trials and let His disciples know that they would face them as well.

- *All troubles happen due to sin or a lack of faith.* Sin does cause problems, and so can a lack of faith. But by no means are those the only two reasons for problems. We have an adversary, the devil, who has made it his goal to destroy the work of God and all who choose to follow Him. Additionally, the Lord many times uses troubles to test us, to develop us, and to glorify himself. And sometimes, troubles simply happen and we may never know why.

- *If we pray, God will remove all of our troubles.* Many times in Scripture we see people who prayed, but their challenges didn't just disappear. In the case of martyrs, they went to their death, and obviously, God didn't remove their problems. The Christian life simply doesn't work this way. We serve an all-powerful, sovereign God who can certainly remove any trouble, and sometimes He does. More often, though, He gives us a way to stand up under the pressure. He allows the trouble because it advances His purposes.

Introduction

Jesus' point in talking with His disciples was not to dwell on their problems, but rather to encourage them with the good news that He has overcome the world. He will help His followers handle their troubles. How? Through His Word, our prayers, and the power and presence of His Holy Spirit.

Let me close by referring to the words the apostle Paul penned to the church in Corinth:

Praise be to the God and Father of our Lord Jesus Christ, the Father of compassion and the God of all comfort, who comforts us in all our troubles, so that we can comfort those in any trouble with the comfort we ourselves have received from God. (2 Corinthians 1:3–4)

These verses contain three powerful truths that I trust will encourage you during your own struggles.

- *God is compassionate.* He has the capability to show compassion and bring comfort to us in any situation.

- *God knows what we're experiencing.* He understands our struggles and hurts, and desires to help us.

- *Our comfort enables us to comfort others.* God doesn't provide His comfort for our sake alone. This verse tells us that as He comforts us, we will be able to comfort others.

Every devotion in this volume is anchored to a Scripture verse in an effort to apply God's truth to some kind of stress, storm, or trouble we encounter in daily life. I've tried to select issues common for people in the military community. God's Word is powerful. If you read and apply God's truth to your own life, I'm confident you'll improve in the way you handle problems.

Would you join me in a brief prayer?

Lord,

I pray that each person who reads this devotional will turn to You in his or her time of trouble. As they do, may You grant them the wisdom, courage, and comfort they need to handle the stress in ways that honor You. And, Lord, as they gain support from You, I pray that You will enable them to supply others with the same comfort You have provided to them.

I pray in Jesus' name. Amen.

— *Scott McChrystal*

Note: Judy and I have collaborated extensively in writing this devotional. All references to "I" or "we" represent our collective efforts and opinions. ■

Christian growth and maturity require consistent effort. If you make this book part of your spiritual fitness plan, you will find it is most useful when read each day. Each daily devotion should take about five minutes to read.

Each volume of *Daily Strength for the Battle*:

- Contains seven weeks of devotions, one devotion per day.

- Each week relates to one theme.

- Each weekly theme begins with a practical illustration designed to demonstrate the relevance and importance of each theme.

- All daily devotions incorporate topics related to the weekly theme.

- All daily devotions begin with a Bible verse related to the topic.

A suggested way to approach your devotional time could include the following:

- Prayer: Ask the Lord to open your heart and mind to the truth of His Word.

- Read the verse at the beginning of the devotion and then paraphrase it in your own words.

- Read the devotional.

- Try to answer the following questions:

  What biblical truth does this devotion talk about?
  How is the truth applied in the devotion?
  Do I believe this truth could be important for my own life?
  How can I apply this truth to my own life?

- Close in prayer: Ask God to help you integrate this truth into your own life.

Five minutes a day may not seem like much, but you can experience wonderful growth in your Christian life by consistently using these short devotions. The Lord will honor your efforts to honor Him. ■

Storms Will Come

*A furious squall came up, and the waves broke
over the boat, so that it was nearly swamped.
Jesus was in the stern, sleeping on a cushion. The
disciples woke him and said to him,
"Teacher, don't you care if we drown?"
(Mark 4:37–38)*

Storms happen in life. Many of them hit suddenly and
with much more force than we ever expect.

The United States has experienced some incredible
storms and natural disasters over the past several years.
Perhaps the one most vividly etched in people's minds is
Hurricane Katrina.

On the morning of August 28, 2005, the National
Weather Service issued an ominous-sounding alert
that would affect the large port city of New Orleans.
Hurricane Katrina, previously listed as a category 1
storm, had suddenly morphed into a category 5 hurricane
heading straight for New Orleans. The prediction went
on to include extensive damage to homes and commercial
buildings, power outages, and widespread flooding. Water
shortages were anticipated as well. All in all, the people of
New Orleans could expect a prolonged time of suffering.

By daybreak of August 29, the cable news coverage
revealed that Katrina was in fact the most damaging

hurricane in U.S. history. Worse yet, the physical damage was not the only challenge. Looting, crime, rape, and sniper fire all joined the mix. Most Americans will never forget the scenes on television. The residents of New Orleans certainly won't.

But know what? Six years later, New Orleans is still on the map. The New Orleans Saints won a Super Bowl and the residents of New Orleans have continued to demonstrate amazing resiliency. Granted, there is much left to do, but the city continues to move forward. Katrina may have been one of the worst disasters in the last hundred years, but that still isn't enough to keep the courageous people of New Orleans down.

Katrina provides us with valuable lessons. One is that life's storms often hit quickly with little or no warning. Another is that the damage from a storm can be worse than predicted. No one expected the 17th Street Canal or other structures controlling water flow in the city to disintegrate, causing massive flooding.

But the critical teaching point is this: What happens to us is not the key issue. What matters most is our response. We don't have much control over circumstances. However, we do get to choose how we will react to the situation.

Let's briefly examine one storm that the disciples experienced. They never anticipated what was coming. Earlier one evening, Jesus had told them to get into some boats and head to the other side of the Sea of Galilee. No biggie — they had done this many times. In fact, some of the disciples were professional fishermen who had spent their entire lives fishing in this water.

Soon after setting out, a windstorm arose — a big one. The geography surrounding the Sea of Galilee includes mountains. Sometimes winds can whip up suddenly from the eastern mountains and make the water appear as though it is boiling in a caldron. This storm was a nasty one and apparently, life-threatening. Surely the fishermen in the group like Peter and John had weathered many storms on this lake. But that night, the situation was simply terrifying, enough so that the disciples feared for their lives.

Yes, the storms of life will come. They will come suddenly, and there is usually nothing we can do to change them. It's not about being a good or bad person. It happens to all of us. The only thing we can do is respond. My mind flashes back to dozens of times I have been with people who have just been hit by a storm. Some reacted well, some panicked, and others remained in denial.

One particular situation sticks out in my mind. LTC John Luther was an outstanding Army officer.

We were stationed together at West Point in the late 1990s. He was a special staff officer to the Superintendent; I was the senior chaplain. One day John got the news he had liver cancer, and it was well advanced.

Over the next three to four months, I spent considerable time with him, and some with his wife, Susan, and son, Caleb. They were Christians, but I totally underestimated the depth of their faith. Sometimes I would accompany John to the doctor to help him through getting fluids drained from his stomach. The surgeon would numb the area, painful enough in itself. Then he would insert a 6-inch needle into John's abdomen and drain off as much as a quart of fluid. And never so much as a peep from John. He was a warrior. Braveheart had nothing on him.

The weeks went by, and John's condition worsened rapidly. Only a miracle could save him. It never came. I remember the funeral service and burial well. It was a privilege to talk about his strong faith.

The outcomes from life's storms don't always go the way we want. But even in situations like the Luther family experienced, the Lord worked many things about those circumstances for good. Caleb, though still young, has strong faith in God as he moves ahead with his life. Susan has dealt with John's passing in positive ways and continues to pursue her life with hope and joy.

At this point, I imagine you have thought about a few of your own storms and how you handled them.

Perhaps you are passing through a storm now. It could be a storm involving health, work, relationships, finances, addictions, depression — virtually anything. It's not so much what the storm is, but rather how you react. Remember, you're not helpless and you get to choose how you will respond.

Let's get back to Jesus and the disciples. His followers are afraid for their lives, but Jesus is sleeping on a pillow in the boat. He hasn't even awakened yet. But the disciples were about to change that. They wake Jesus up and start in with a pretty harsh line of questioning: "Teacher, don't you care if we drown?"

Jesus was not caught off guard. He gets up and does two things. First, He rebukes the wind and the waves by saying, "Peace, be still!" To the disciples' amazement, the winds cease and the sea suddenly becomes calm. God can still do that, you know.

But note what happened next. Jesus answers the disciples' questions with a couple of His own: "Why are you so fearful? How is it that you have no faith?"

We know from Jesus' life that He was a man of compassion, but in this case, that was not His approach. He called them to account. First, Jesus wanted to know why the disciples were so fearful. And then He questioned them about their faith — where was it?

Often I wish the Gospel writers had told us more. We never learn how the disciples responded to those questions. We do know that they became even more fearful as they asked each other, "Who is this guy? Even the wind and sea follow His orders."

And we know something else. They continued to follow Jesus — even to their dying breath.

So how might this story impact you as you consider your response to life's storms? Let me suggest several ways.

First, where was Jesus during this storm? Answer: He was right there in their midst. Granted, He was sleeping for a while and didn't intervene. But He was there. And where has He been during your storms? Yes, right there with you! He always has been and always will be. That is His promise to believers.

Second, as the disciples woke Him and voiced their fears, Jesus listened and understood their concerns. He answered their prayer with supernatural power. In your storms, you can count on the Lord listening and understanding. He may not do a miracle to solve the problem instantaneously, but He will answer. You can count on that.

Finally, consider the questions Jesus posed to the disciples? Granted, it was a legitimately life-threatening situation. But Jesus asked why they were so fearful. He wanted to know why they exercised no faith.

Jesus was making the point that the disciples didn't need to fall apart in this circumstance. They didn't need to panic. Instead, they should have noted that Jesus was there with them and simply exercised their faith.

Could it be that the Lord wants you to remember these same truths when storms come into your life?

Just as Jesus asked His disciples about their faith, He challenges us to use our faith. We've all seen the Lord act in our lives many times. Why should it be any different when the next storm comes our way? The answer is simple. It won't. The God of the universe is always with us, and He can do anything.

Not to worry. God is present. Exercise your faith. ∎

When Trouble Comes Your Way

"I have told you these things, so that in me you may have peace. In this world you will have trouble. But take heart! I have overcome the world."
(John 16:33)

Daily we are bombarded with offers to lessen stress in our lives: new cars, great foods, laborsaving devices, and magical medications. All claim in some way that they will remove stress from the hectic grind of our busy schedules.

But have you noticed that stress levels in society continue to rise, not fall? In many cases, these offers don't lower stress. They raise it!

Hoping to eliminate stress from life is a pipe dream. Jesus would agree. In this verse, He lays out two truths related to stress. First, He says as long as we live in this world, we will have troubles. It's a given.

Secondly, He doesn't promise to remove all stress. But He tells us to take heart. He has overcome the world. Though we will always have stressors, Jesus will be there to support us.

Real peace is not the absence of stress, but rather the presence of God in your life. Don't face your stress alone. Let God help. ∎

God Allows Stress for Our Good

And we know that in all things God works for the good of those who love him, who have been called according to his purpose.
(Romans 8:28)

Adversity is not the enemy of good. With the right perspective, it can be an ally.

There is a story about an eagle who complained to his fellow eagle: "If it weren't for the air, I could fly faster!" Not! Without air, the eagle couldn't leave the ground.

Don't we think like this sometimes? Our perspective is limited. God's is not. He allows us to experience trials that He knows will help us, not hurt us. In this verse, Paul tells the Christians in Rome that God doesn't waste an experience. He works it all together for good.

Note two points here:

- It doesn't say everything is good. Rather, God works things together for good.
- God does this for those who love Him and are trying to follow His purposes.

Don't dread stress and adversity. God can work it for your good. ■

Better Days Are Coming!

And the God of all grace, who called you to his eternal glory in Christ, after you have suffered a little while, will himself restore you and make you strong, firm and steadfast.
(1 Peter 5:10)

As I walked into his hospital room, it was obvious the young paratrooper was feeling lower than dirt. He had contracted a rare virus while training in Central America. The doctors ordered the right medicine, but the medical logistical system just wasn't being responsive.

Rarely have I ever witnessed anyone suffer more. Day after day, his desperation grew more intense. He was losing perspective.

Fortunately, I was able to encourage the soldier with verses from God's Word. One of them was this verse found in 1 Peter. It provides perspective during times of distress by reminding us that the suffering won't last forever. The Lord will restore us and make us strong.

The soldier took this truth to heart and gained courage to face his sickness. After almost a month, the medicine arrived. In just a few days he returned back to normal.

Remember this: Suffering may last for a season, but God will restore you. Better days are coming! ■

You're Not the Only One

No temptation has overtaken you except what is common to mankind. And God is faithful; he will not let you be tempted beyond what you can bear. But when you are tempted, he will also provide a way out so that you can endure it.
(1 Corinthians 10:13)

The old saying that "misery loves company" does contain some truth. When we are under great stress or trial, it's comforting to know that others are facing or have experienced similar pressures.

Simply knowing that we're not the only ones going through tough times can help us maintain perspective. Perspective involves seeing the big picture and not allowing specific details of our lives to warp our view. I like this humorous saying about perspective: "There's only one thing worse than a flooded basement, and that's a flooded attic."

Does it feel like the attic of your life is flooded? Are you experiencing hard times — relationally, emotionally, financially, spiritually, or in some other way?

Take heart, my friend. This Scripture reminds us that God knows your situation. Others have gone through similar situations. It's not hopeless. He helped others. He will make a way for you to make it! ■

Remember What God Has Done

"The LORD who rescued me from the paw of the lion and the paw of the bear will rescue me from the hand of this Philistine."
(1 Samuel 17:37)

Remembering the past helps us keep perspective.

Picture the scene. A teenage boy is pleading his case before the king of Israel. A godless giant named Goliath has defied both the armies of mighty Israel and the God they serve. No Israelite warrior has mustered the courage to fight Goliath one-on-one — except David.

King Saul is certain David is volunteering himself for a suicide mission. David is a brave boy, but no match for this Philistine killing machine. And besides, if David loses to Goliath, Israel loses as well. Risky business.

At some time during the conversation, David gives Saul a riveting stare along with words to this effect. "Look, King Saul, God has delivered from the lion and bear. Our mighty God will deliver me from this ugly bully as well."

That did it. Saul saw that David wasn't hallucinating. He had perspective solidly grounded on what God had done before.

Don't forget. God has done mighty things in your life. And He will again! ∎

Don't Trust Your Feelings

> *We are hard pressed on every side, but*
> *not crushed; perplexed, but not in despair;*
> *persecuted, but not abandoned; struck down,*
> *but not destroyed.*
> *(2 Corinthians 4:8–9)*

Erwin Lutzer, nationally known pastor and author, nailed it when he said: "A Christian life based on feeling is headed for a gigantic collapse."

Do we ignore our feelings? Absolutely not. But neither are we to base our decisions upon how we feel. We'd never accomplish anything worthwhile if we let that happen.

A year ago, I was visiting Fort Benning, Georgia. I had been asked to visit a young soldier in Basic Combat Training who was having a rough time. He was only a few days from graduation but had contracted a dose of the flu and felt rotten.

He asked me what he should do. He was hoping I would tell him to quit. I didn't. Instead I encouraged him to "lean forward in the foxhole" and not let his feelings drive his decision.

Weeks later, I received a wonderful e-mail from his uncle along with a picture of the young trooper in his Class A uniform. He had made it.

The apostle Paul's advice in this verse is right. Drive on! ■

Claim God's Promises

*Abraham reasoned that God could even raise the
dead, and so in a manner of speaking he did receive
Isaac back from death.*
(Hebrews 11:19)

The Bible claims that God can do anything. Do you
keep that perspective as you live your life?

Abraham did. This verse makes reference to the time
when God commanded this patriarch to sacrifice his son.

A little background helps here. Barren all of her adult
life, Abraham's wife, Sarah, was told by the Lord that
she would have a son when she was 90 years old. God
kept His promise and Sarah delivered Isaac.

When Isaac became a teenager, God gave this
seemingly strange order to sacrifice him. You don't
even have to be a parent to imagine how hard this must
have been for Abraham and Sarah — off the chart.

But look what happened. Abraham obeyed. He
remembered God's promise to make him the father
of many nations. This verse tells us that "Abraham
reasoned that God could even raise the dead, and so in
a manner of speaking he did receive Isaac back from
death."

Going through hard times — maybe the toughest
you've ever faced? Claim God's promises. He delivers! ∎

Shipwrecked

When neither sun nor stars appeared for many days and the storm continued raging, we finally gave up all hope of being saved. . . . So keep up your courage, men, for I have faith in God that it will happen just as he told me.
(Acts 27:20,25)

Human responses to impending danger vary widely. It's difficult to know how those around you will act. Until it happens, we can't really know how we ourselves will behave.

I think back to September 11, 2001, a day that will live in our memories. Chances are you can remember exactly where you were and what you were doing when you first got the news about the planes hitting the North and South towers of the World Trade Center.

Most of America witnessed the responses by fellow citizens in New York City. Following the crash of American Airlines Flight 11 into the North Tower at 8:46 AM, most wondered how the plane could have strayed so far off course. At 9:03 AM, when United Flight 175 crashed into the South Tower at 590 miles per hour, we quickly realized that the United States was under attack.

We witnessed brave policemen and firemen, along with other citizens, spring into action to help those in distress. Once the South Tower crashed around 9:59 AM, we saw people trapped on the upper floors of the North Tower making the decision to leap to their death. Others trapped inside made final phone calls to loved ones. Still others frantically searched for escape routes to lower floors. More than likely, others froze in place or prayed in their final minutes of life.

But America soon learned that the terrorist plot encompassed more than New York City. Those at the Pentagon reacted quickly to evacuate victims hurt or killed when American Flight 77 crashed into the western side of the building.

Perhaps, though, the travelers on United Flight 93 faced the chilling effects of terrorism in the most personal and in-your-face manner. Following takeover of American Airlines Flight 93, passengers on board rapidly pieced bits of information together to discover that their plane was on a suicide mission to the Washington, D.C., area. In a heroic effort to prevent more killing, Todd Beamer and several other passengers stormed the flight cabin, overwhelming the hijackers, leaving the plane with no one in control. The giant jet crashed into a field in Sumerset County, Pennsylvania, west of Pittsburgh. No survivors.

Ten years following 9/11, America is still responding. Of course, many associated with the military continue to be directly impacted by decisions stemming from the terrorist attacks. War in Iraq and Afghanistan continues, and multiplied thousands of servicemen and women have served or still serve in harm's way. Their families and loved ones share in their sacrifices.

The rest of us, in one way or another, have made choices that affect how we remember and process the traumatic events of that day. These decisions also impact our future — how we think and behave as we move ahead collectively and individually.

I've intentionally selected 9/11 to get you thinking about stress and the wide range of options for responding to it. Stress is a reality, and it's critical that each of us learn some things about adversity and stress, particularly how we personally respond in these kinds of situations.

We're not robots; we do have the capacity to choose. But learning to make healthy choices is not automatic. We need to understand the impacts of trauma and stress, and learn from the past. Assessing the behavior of others along with our own responses to stress can be helpful as well. We can explore alternative ways to handle stress and compare the merits of each. All in all, there has never been more information available.

But let me suggest another source for coping with stress, and there is nothing new about this approach. It simply involves placing our faith in God.

Doubtlessly, you remember the role of faith during 9/11. I personally can't remember a time when our nation turned to God for strength, guidance, and support as much as during this period of national crisis. While some still seek God for help, most Americans have returned to their normal schedule, one that includes much less conscious dependence upon the Lord. I'm not trying to be critical. This is simply the way it is.

The question for each of us is not whether we will face trauma and crisis in the future. The issue is how we will respond. Are you satisfied with the way you handle stress? Do you think and act in ways that are healthy and constructive? What do others say about you during times of stress? When periods of confusion and chaos happen, do you help or hinder? When trouble strikes, what sort of example do you set for your spouse or children? Overall, how are you coping with stress as you consider the future?

Regardless of how well or how poorly you handle stress, you can get better. You can help others around you deal with their pressures more effectively. How? By learning to trust God in tight situations. God has been helping people since Adam and Eve. He's just as willing to help you.

Consider an incident in the apostle Paul's life. He was a Roman prisoner on his way to Rome to get a hearing with the Emperor Nero. Under the care of a Roman centurion, he and 275 other men boarded an Alexandrian ship bound for Italy. Paul sensed that setting sail at this time was not advisable, and he warned the centurion and the ship's crew that sailing at that time could jeopardize their lives. His advice was ignored. They set out for the island of Crete, hoping to harbor there for the winter.

Although the weather was initially mild, it deteriorated rapidly. Soon they found themselves in a violent winter storm with no ability to control their direction. Over the next few days, the crew started throwing all unnecessary weight overboard in an effort to lighten the ship. Days passed with no change. Survival appeared unlikely.

Luke summed up the situation in verse 20: "We finally gave up all hope of being saved." Luke was not the only one. Apparently everyone else on board had the same perception — that is, except Paul, who had a quite different view. He stood up and addressed everyone on the ship. He told how an angel of God had visited him and assured Paul that he would make it safely to Rome. The angel also indicated that everyone on board would survive as well.

Paul believed the angel's words and shared his faith and hope with the others. He gave them instructions and told everyone to eat something to gain strength for the ordeal they were about to experience. Just as Paul predicted, the ship ran aground as they approached the island of Malta. Miraculously, all on board swam or rode pieces of the ship safely to land. Everyone survived, just as the angel had promised.

Can this story from Paul's life teach us something about handling stress in our lives today? Absolutely. But we must not only learn it, we need to apply it.

First, the storm appeared, posing life-threatening danger to everyone on the ship. It was unavoidable. Many of the traumatic, stress-producing events in our lives can't be avoided. They simply happen.

Secondly, just as those on board the Alexandrian ship got to choose their outlook, so do we. Everyone on the ship, except Paul, viewed the situation by the way it appeared to their natural eye. It truly did seem as though the end was near.

But Paul made a different choice, the choice of faith. Despite the visible evidence all around him, Paul elected to put his trust in God. He assumed a leadership role and was instrumental in saving the lives of everyone on board.

Although it is likely that you are not facing a life versus death situation, stress may still be affecting your life in many negative ways. No one stressor seems to be that bad, but the cumulative effects are making your life miserable. You keep hoping that tomorrow will be a new day. But each morning brings the same stresses, the same negative feelings, and the overall feeling that life is overwhelming you. Chances are you're a stressor for those around you.

Is there hope for you? The answer is yes — definitely! The answer probably won't come in one miraculous step, but in a series of smaller steps that can help you get your life on the right track.

To summarize, consider the following:

- Stress is universal. Everyone experiences it.

- While you can't usually control what happens, you can control your response. You choose.

- It helps to identify the stressors in your life. In doing so, don't simply identify the symptoms. Try to get to the real issues. Seek the help of others you trust to assist you in this process.

- Select one or two stressors to work on. Don't try to tackle everything at once.

- Decide what needs to change and make plans. One caution here: Even if you have tried and failed numerous times previously, don't let your past dictate. Try again!

- Celebrate your successes, but don't get down on yourself if you fall short. Try again. Adjust your plans and expectations if necessary.

- Commit your plans to the Lord. If you do, they will succeed (Proverbs 16:3). ■

Stressed By Threats

Meanwhile, the people in Judah said, "The strength of the laborers is giving out, and there is so much rubble that we cannot rebuild the wall." (Nehemiah 4:10)

Stress induced by combat, or even the threat of combat, is not a new development. Terminology to identify the condition has changed, but the effects have been around for a long time. A common name used today is Post Traumatic Stress (PTS).

Over 2,500 years ago, Nehemiah was leading the effort to rebuild the walls of Jerusalem, spiritual headquarters for Israel. Progress went well up until the halfway point. Then leaders from a few small surrounding nations that felt threatened by Israel's potential resurgence banded together to oppose Nehemiah. Their initial strategy consisted of intimidation through a series of threatening messages, most of which were lies.

The enemy's tactics began working. Sizeable numbers of Israelite citizens became fearful about the future and started to lose hope. Fortunately, Nehemiah chose to trust God. He saw through the enemy's strategy and helped the workers remain focused on the mission.

Be like Nehemiah. Don't let someone's threats stop you. Trust God and stay focused on your mission. The Lord will help you. ■

People React Differently

When the disciples saw him walking on the lake,
they were terrified. "It's a ghost," they said, and
cried out in fear. But Jesus immediately said to
them: "Take courage! It is I. Don't be afraid."
"Lord, if it's you," Peter replied, "tell me
to come to you on the water."
(Matthew 14:26-28)

Have you noticed that people respond differently
in stressful situations? One person responds one way.
Another acts very differently. Determining what's
"normal" is not always easy, or even possible.

Consider the situation as reported in Matthew's Gospel.
The disciples are in a boat on the Sea of Galilee — at
night. Suddenly they see what they believe is a ghost
walking on the water toward their boat. The disciples cry
out in fear.

But get this. After Jesus identifies himself, Peter
requests permission to walk on the water to Jesus! And
he did — until the winds and waves stressed him out
and he began to sink.

Teaching point? There are many, but one is to
recognize and understand how you respond in stressful
situations.

Don't worry so much about what's normal.
Regardless of how you respond, the Lord is always
there to help. ∎

Choosing What's Better

"Martha, Martha," the Lord answered, "you are worried and upset about many things, but few things are needed — or indeed only one. Mary has chosen what is better, and it will not be taken away from her."
(Luke 10:41-42)

Have you ever found yourself stressed out, running in circles, and getting zero help from those around you?

Martha was ticked. Her preparations for the meal were not going well. She was reaching the panic stage. So much needed to be done. Her sister, Mary, was just sitting there with their houseguest, seemingly hanging on to every word Jesus spoke.

Finally, Martha had reached her limit. She blurted out to Jesus, "Tell my sister to help me!"

What happened next must have surprised Martha. Jesus calmly looked at Martha and told her that Mary, not Martha, had made the better choice. Meal preparations could be done anytime. Sitting at Jesus' feet could not.

The story ends before we find out Martha's response. I choose to believe Martha felt convicted and calmed at the same time. Mary had made the better choice.

Instead of getting all stressed out by your circumstances, make a better choice. Give Jesus your undivided attention. ■

Day 4

No Need to Ruin Your Life

Like a city whose walls are broken through
is a person who lacks self-control.
(Proverbs 25:28)

During ancient times, the walls around a city provided major protection against the enemy. If an attacker could destroy the walls, the inhabitants of that city quickly became losers.

At the personal level, our walls can be quickly broken down, particularly if we don't exercise self-control during times of stress.

In the military today, we tend to minimize situations when someone gets stressed, loses control, and curses or throws an object across the room. No big deal, we think. But consequences can range from slight to catastrophic.

A number of years ago, I had to visit one of my troops being held in jail for manslaughter. He was at home and becoming very stressed because his 18-month-old son wouldn't stop crying. The soldier gets the idea to give his child a bath. The kid still wouldn't stop yelling. The young father loses it, and slams the youngster's head against the side of the tub. Tragically, his son suffered a concussion and died.

During times of stress, don't blow your cool. The Lord will help you. ■

How Do You See It?

Then Caleb silenced the people before Moses and said, "We should go up and take possession of the land, for we can certainly do it."
(Numbers 13:30)

Perspective is critical in life. How you view situations can make all the difference.

Do you normally see the glass half empty or half full? Some people tend to be negative, usually seeing the glass half empty. Others choose to see the glass half full.

This verse takes us back to an AAR (After Action Review) from one of the first-ever recorded reconnaissance missions. The twelve Israelite spies couldn't reach consensus. Ten of them told Moses and the people that taking the land of Canaan was simply not doable. The inhabitants were too numerous and too powerful.

Joshua and Caleb saw it differently. Caleb voiced confidence by saying, "We can certainly do it."

What made Joshua and Caleb different? The next chapter provides the answer: "If the LORD is pleased with us, he will lead us into that land, a land flowing with milk and honey, and will give it to us" (Numbers 14:8).

If the Lord gives you a mission to accomplish, simply trust Him and get to work! ■

New Information

*The jailer woke up, and when he saw the prison
doors open, he drew his sword and was about to
kill himself because he thought the
prisoners had escaped.*
(Acts 16:27)

Here's a blunt question: Have you ever seriously
considered suicide? Many of us have. Contemplating
suicide at some point in life is not limited to a select few.

Suicide rates within the military are at an all-time
high. Leaders, both inside and outside the military, are
searching for answers without much success.

Fundamentally, suicide represents the loss of hope. The
jailer in this story lost hope when he thought his prisoners
had escaped following an earthquake that opened prison
doors. Figuring that he faced certain death at the hands
of Roman soldiers for failing in his mission, the jailer was
about to commit suicide.

But Paul came to the rescue, shouting out to the jailer
that all prisoners were still present. Armed with new
information, hope quickly returned for the jailer.

Whenever you feel down and your hope is melting
away, remember the jailer. New information restored his
hope and helped him to regain perspective.

God stands ready with new information that will
restore your hope. Just ask Him! ■

Help for Serious Stress

In her deep anguish Hannah prayed to the LORD, weeping bitterly.
(1 Samuel 1:10)

Have you ever experienced hurt or stress so deep that it brought anguish to the core of your being? Sooner or later most of us do.

Hannah was an Old Testament woman who had not been able to have children. In Hebrew culture, providing male offspring for the sake of continuing the family was of special significance. The woman who could not bear a son was considered to have brought shame to her husband.

We know from this verse that Hannah prayed to the Lord in bitterness of soul. Words couldn't adequately describe her pain.

But take careful note as to how she dealt with her stress. She didn't deny it, try to self-medicate, or drown her sorrows with alcohol. Rather, she sought the Lord in heartfelt prayer. God heard her prayer and answered it. A short time later she became pregnant and bore a son named Samuel.

In times when stress brings anguish to your soul, remember Hannah. Don't let stress take you down. Take your cares to God in prayer.

He will answer you. ■

Tempted to Give Up

Elijah was afraid and ran for his life. When he came to Beersheba in Judah, he left his servant there, while he himself went a day's journey into the wilderness. He came to a broom bush, sat down under it and prayed that he might die. "I have had enough, LORD," he said. "Take my life; I am no better than my ancestors."
(1 Kings 19:3–4)

It has been said that "stress is the spice of life; we just don't want to get over spiced." Today many have become "over spiced," and the impact has been negative. Too many people are giving up, and some of them belong to the military community.

Don't be among those who allow themselves to be overwhelmed and just throw in the towel. You can make it!

Given the 10 years of war in Iraq and Afghanistan, the military community has been at the tip of the spear when it comes to facing stressful situations. The cumulative negative effects have been wide-ranging and widespread — from the battlefield to the home front. Warriors represent the group most affected, but it hardly stops with them. Spouses, children, relatives, friends, community members — all have felt the effects of stress to varying degrees.

This section of our devotional book deals with the negative impacts of stress and attempts to highlight a few of the most common effects. There are many more, but it will help us make some general observations that apply to most situations.

Obviously, the most commonly used terms related to stress on the battlefield are Post Traumatic Stress (PTS) and Post Traumatic Stress Disorder (PTSD). It is well documented that many of our service men and women have experienced stress associated with combat. Research continues to explore the causes and treatment.

But it would be a mistake to lump too much in with PTS/PTSD. As we've said before, stress is universal. There are plenty of signs telling us that US society is not handling stress well. Ironically, I believe that some of our so-called stress relievers are actually compounding the problem.

Remember, stress is nothing new. It's as old as mankind. Though we are constantly finding out new things through research, the Bible has many things to tell us that don't represent recent discoveries. These are truths that applied in the past and continue into the present.

Take the story of Elijah at Mount Carmel. It provides a fascinating account of a brave warrior standing up to a seemingly impossible challenge. At the same time, it demonstrates the frailty of mankind when we reach our limits — and everyone has limits.

By the 9th century B.C., Israel was a divided kingdom —
northern and southern. The Northern Kingdom consisted
of ten tribes that largely had abandoned worship of Yahweh
and began worshipping the pagan gods of Baal. The
reigning king of the Northern Kingdom was a man named
Ahab, an evil king. His wife, Jezebel, was a woman from
Phoenicia steeped in pagan worship and who financially
supported hundreds of priests and prophets of Baal.

Along comes Elijah, a prophet of God. In an attempt to
combat false religions, he challenged 450 prophets of Baal
and 400 prophets of Asherah to a contest to determine
whose God really had power. He challenged the people of
Israel to choose whom they would follow — Baal or God.
The contest consisted of building two altars and placing a
sacrificial animal on each altar. The god who answered by
fire would be acclaimed as the true God.

The prophets of Baal went first, calling out to their
god and dancing before the altar. As the hours passed,
some even slashed themselves with swords and spears.
There was plenty of blood. But fire never came. As
evening approached, Elijah continued to taunt them in
a loud voice. The prophets of Baal were exhausted, but
still no fire.

Now it was Elijah's turn. He fixed the altar of the
Lord, adding twelve stones to it, one for each of the tribes
of Israel. Then he dug a trench around the altar, piled
wood on it, and placed pieces of a bull to be used as the
sacrifice. Finally, he poured large jars of water on the
altar. He repeated this twice more.

Now, the moment of decision.
Praying to the Lord, Elijah
concluded his prayer: "Answer me,
LORD, answer me, so these people
will know that you, LORD, are
God, and that you are turning their hearts back
again."

Talk about setting himself up! If God chose
not to answer Elijah's prayer, he was toast. He
was outnumbered hundreds to one.

But God did answer Elijah's prayer,
immediately and by fire. The fire consumed the
sacrifice, the wood, the stones, and the water. All
present cried out in unison, "The LORD — he is
God! The LORD — he is God!"

What happened next was not pretty. Elijah ordered the
450 prophets of Baal to be taken to the Kishon Valley and
slaughtered. This action would quickly have consequences
for Elijah. As soon as King Ahab told Jezebel about the
slaughter, she sent a message to Elijah announcing she
would have him killed in the next 24 hours.

By this time, Elijah felt exhausted. The stress and strain
of his encounter with the false prophets had taken its
toll — mentally, physically, emotionally, and spiritually.
Jezebel's message triggered fear in Elijah's heart, and his
first instinct was to run.

He ran to Beersheba in Judah, and leaving his servant
there, traveled a day's journey into the desert. The

adrenalin rush that propelled his initial flight was over. He was running on fumes. He came to a broom bush and collapsed. He then prayed to the Lord. Notice the contents of his prayer.

First, he said, "I have had enough, LORD." Who among us can't identify with that statement? Can you remember feeling that way and repeating almost those exact words? The stresses and pressures of life can close in on us like walls. We get to the point where we feel we can't take it any more. Something has to change.

What happens after those feelings hit you? In Elijah's case, we know exactly what happened. He continued his prayer, "Take my life; I am no better than my ancestors."

Do you realize who this man was and what he was saying here? Elijah was a great prophet of God. The Lord had just used him to win the victory over hundreds of false prophets. It is hard to imagine how Elijah could have been more bold or courageous for God. But he had reached his limit.

Finally, in asking God to take his life, Elijah made a confession — and it was the truth. He realized that he was a mere mortal, a man no better and no worse than those who had gone before him. He realized that he was a frail and weak human being subject to the same vulnerabilities as other men.

Fortunately for Elijah, the story doesn't end here. Read the rest of 1 Kings 19 for yourself. An angel visits Elijah, feeds him, and tells him to go to Mount Horeb to meet

with God. At Horeb, God speaks
to Elijah and helps the exhausted
prophet to regain his strength, his
perspective, and his faith. Elijah is
able to regroup and continue his
ministry as a prophet.

Let's apply a few things from Elijah's life
that can help us deal with tough times. First,
sooner or later most people will encounter
stress that threatens to overwhelm them. If you
are associated with the military, that time will
probably happen sooner. So don't feel like you're
the only one who has ever felt this way.

Second, Elijah let his feelings govern his
response to the situation. For a brief time, he
simply lost his head. He also lost his perspective.
His hope tank registered empty. In this context, he asked
God to take his life.

Most of us, if we are honest, have been at this same
place. We've wondered why life is so hard and have
thought that continuing to live isn't worth the pain. We
may have contemplated suicide and even started to make
plans.

Third, what stresses you to the point of giving up may
not be what stresses someone else. We're all different.
You may be thinking, "I can handle a fire fight or an
explosion from an IED (Improvised Explosive Device),
but this marriage thing is driving me insane." Continuing

further, you deal with a lot of hard stuff, but somehow it seems like little things are driving you over the edge.

Bottom line: It really doesn't matter what causes your stress. The point is that you have to decide that you will not give up. Never. Just as God came to Elijah's rescue by sending an angel, He will come to your aid as well. God helped to restore Elijah's strength and perspective. He can do the same for you.

Let faith arise within you. Make up your mind now that you and God together can deal with any situation that will happen. Determine that no matter how tough things get, you will not give up.

If you learn to approach life with this outlook, you'll discover that fear will melt and your faith will grow. Your joy and zest for life will increase as well. And that's just the way the Lord wants it. ■

Dismayed and Terrified

*On hearing the Philistine's words, Saul and all the
Israelites were dismayed and terrified.*
(1 Samuel 17:11)

Stress can produce many adverse effects, one of which is
fear. This kind of fear is often characterized by a host of other
symptoms:

- Loss of perspective
- Erosion of confidence
- Negative self-talk
- Diminished capability to focus
- Tendency toward panic
- Paralysis in normal ability to act

The Philistine giant named Goliath made daily threats to
the Israelite army. Every soldier froze in fear. Nobody dared
to move a muscle in response to Goliath's challenge to fight.

But there is good news. As people of God, we don't have
to let stress paralyze us with fear. Our faith in an Almighty
God can melt our fears and provide the courage we need for
the situation.

David was only a young shepherd boy at the time, but he
knew the Lord would help him prevail against Goliath. God
would fight the battle for him. David killed the giant and
later became king of all Israel.

Don't let that giant called stress defeat you. Identify the
giant, go after him, and trust God for your victory. ■

Day 2

Loss of Perspective

O God, why have you rejected us forever?
Why does your anger smolder against the sheep
of your pasture?
(Psalm 74:1)

It's just part of the human condition. When bad things happen and seem to keep happening, we are prone to lose our perspective. The Psalmist certainly had. This opening verse of Psalm 74 accuses God of having rejected Israel forever.

Was the accusation true? No — absolutely not. But for the writer, it felt that way. Israel had sinned for decades. Present circumstances merely reflected the consequences of disobedience. Jerusalem was in shambles and enemies were gloating.

I visited a young warrior in the hospital who felt God was rejecting him. He was in a funk, and I could hardly blame him. Major skin graft surgery on his left thigh wasn't working. Weeks went by with no progress.

One day, we were together and he broke down in tears, weeping bitterly. I agreed with him in prayer as he poured his heart out to God. A few days later, healing began. In a few weeks, he had made full recovery.

God had not rejected him after all. Neither will God reject you. ∎

When Depression Strikes

I am bowed down and brought very low;
all day long I go about mourning.
(Psalm 38:6)

Depression is no respecter of persons. It can strike anyone. If you have never experienced a prolonged season of depression, consider yourself fortunate. But don't assume it can't happen to you.

David was a man after God's own heart, but he experienced times of severe depression. Note David's words about himself: "all day long I go about mourning."

What triggers depression? Many things. David was under constant attack by his enemies, both physical and verbal. Additionally, even his family and friends were avoiding him during his time of suffering and pain.

But David didn't allow depression to destroy him. In his desperation he sought the Lord. God heard his prayers and restored him.

Depression is widespread here in America. Just look at the ads on TV for medications that claim to help combat it.

Sometimes medication is genuinely needed. But God is our best medicine. He can help you identify the root causes of your depression and heal you from the inside out.

Depressed? Talk with God about it. ∎

Burn Out

He came to a broom bush, sat down under it and
prayed that he might die. "I have had enough,
LORD," he said. "Take my life."
(1 Kings 19:4)

He was a decorated war hero. During combat in Iraq, he earned valorous awards along with the reputation as a future military leader at the highest levels.

Upon his return to the United States, his life began to unravel. Though outwardly he was flourishing, some PTSD issues started to take a toll on him and on his family. He tried to self-medicate and managed to hide most of his struggles. Gradually, however, those around him saw dangerous warning signs. He was on the brink of burnout.

Finally, a senior officer in his chain of command directed that he seek medical help. This courageous decision probably saved the young officer's life, his family, and his career.

Elijah prayed that he might die. The Lord used an angel to comfort the dejected prophet. In the situation above, God used a senior military officer to intervene.

Are you headed for burnout? Don't try to handle the situation by yourself. Ask the God of this universe to rescue you. He understands you and will provide the support you need. ∎

No One to Help Me

*"Sir," the invalid replied, "I have no one
to help me into the pool when the water is stirred.
While I am trying to get in, someone else goes
down ahead of me."*
(John 5:7)

Hopelessness is a very dangerous place. Name the circumstances. Take hope away and there's not much chance for a good outcome.

One day Jesus came upon a man who met this description. The poor guy had been an invalid for 38 years. Jesus asked the man an interesting question: "Do you want to get well?"

The man's answer reflected his hopelessness. Though the invalid was only feet away from a pool purported to have healing power, he told Jesus, "I have no one to help me into the pool."

Yes, the man was hopeless. But why? The invalid mistakenly placed his faith in a pool with supposed healing powers. Little did the man realize that on this day, he was staring into the face of the Creator of the universe. Jesus spoke. The invalid was instantly healed.

Is your hope tank on empty? Marriage, health, finances, career, loneliness — it doesn't matter. When you place your trust in God, no situation is hopeless. ■

Day 6

Suicidal Thoughts

*When Zimri saw that the city was taken, he went
into the citadel of the royal palace and set the
palace on fire around him. So he died.*
(1 Kings 16:18)

Suicide is not a new issue. Zimri was a king in ancient
Bible times. When the army of Israel laid siege to his town,
he saw no way out. He set fire to his palace and remained
until his death.

Taking one's own life is the ultimate tragedy. From the
individual's point of view, leaving this world seems like the
only way out. But it's not, and it never is.

So how do we make certain we don't make this fatal
decision? First, recognize that the stresses of life can feel
overwhelming to any of us. No one is immune. Second,
decide now that suicide is never an alternative for your
life. Even though thoughts of suicide are not uncommon,
decide now that you will never exercise this option.

And don't just think about yourself. Suicide of a loved
one devastates a spouse, family, and friends.

Finally, remember that your life is precious to God. He
gave you life. When the walls of your world seem to close
in around you, cry out to God. He will rescue you. That's
just what He does. ■

Where Is God?

He trusts in God. Let God rescue him now if he wants him, for he said, "I am the Son of God." (Matthew 27:43)

Stress can do damaging things to our faith, and no one is immune.

During the darkest moments of life's storms, it can seem difficult or even impossible to sense God's presence. All of us remember the scenes from 9/11 and the horrible images of death and destruction. Many who lost loved ones asked the question, "Where is God?"

I've been in many situations where that question was asked — death of a spouse or child, the loss of a fellow soldier in combat, or the death of a coworker due to a sudden heart attack.

It's a common question, and one that was even uttered as Jesus was dying on the cross. In this case it was the religious leaders, not Jesus, who asked the question.

During these excruciatingly stressful moments, we demand action from God. We want to see him act quickly to change the situation.

But we can't let our feelings dictate. At the very worst of times, the Lord says to each of us, "Don't be afraid. I am right here with you." ■

Marine Steps Up to Next Level

Not only so, but we also glory in our sufferings, because we know that suffering produces perseverance; perseverance, character; and character, hope.
(Romans 5:3–4)

Trials come to all of us. While we don't exercise control over many of the situations that occur in life, there is one thing for sure: We get to choose how we respond.

I have experienced suffering in my own life from time to time. We all have. Can't say that I am a big fan of it, but I must admit that enormous good has come out of the trials I've faced.

How about you? How do you view the adversity that you've experienced? Although you might not want to repeat those times, can you see how God has worked suffering for good in your life?

The veteran missionary, Paul, wrote these verses to Christians in Rome. He was trying to encourage them with respect to the persecution and suffering they were facing as Christians under pagan rule. Note that he tells them that he rejoices in his sufferings.

Wow! Why would he do that? Paul had been beaten several times within an inch of his life, stoned and left for dead, and shipwrecked on numerous occasions. He knew what hardship and suffering looked like.

But Paul answers the question as to why he rejoiced: It was because of what the suffering had produced. Through tough times, he had developed perseverance. Perseverance produced character, and character gave him hope. As Christians we need all three: perseverance, character, and hope.

Let me tell you about a friend of mine who has rebounded from trials about as well as any individual I personally know. His name is Clebe McClary, a Marine. I first met Clebe in 1985 when I was serving as a chaplain in the 82nd Airborne Division. I was responsible for two battalions at the time and invited him to be a guest speaker for both units. Clebe's autobiography, *Living Proof*, tells the entire story, but let me briefly relate a few things about the trial he experienced.

First Lieutenant McClary was serving as a platoon leader with the First Marine Division's First Reconnaissance Battalion. The year was 1968 and the place was South Vietnam just south of An Hoa. On March 3, 1Lt. McClary's 13-man team was occupying positions on Hill 146 in preparation for a large operation that was to occur in a few days. Upon arrival at the location, they quickly discovered that the enemy had tried to turn the football-sized area into a death trap through a series of booby traps and pungi pits.

The team cleared the mines, pungi pits, and other explosives on the hill. Soon after, they learned that the large operation had been cancelled, and that helicopters would extract them as soon as the weather cleared. On the third night on Hill 146, 1Lt. McClary's life on this earth would be radically changed.

The team knew they were being watched by elements of the North Vietnamese Army (NVA), but they had no idea what was about to happen. Around midnight, large numbers of NVA soldiers along with a sapper element attacked their positions with a barrage of rifle fire, grenades, and satchel charges.

If you want to hear the account in detail, I recommend you buy his book. But for now let me simply say that 10 of the 13 Marines were either killed or wounded, one of those being 1Lt. McClary. Miraculously, rescue helicopters were able to pull the team off Hill 146 before everyone was killed.

Clebe's injuries were bad — life-threatening for several days. For a starter, a grenade had blown off his left arm above the elbow. His left eye had been blown out. He sustained shrapnel wounds over most of his body. Bottom line: He was a mess.

I'll finish telling you more about Clebe shortly, but I must pause to tell you about Deanna, his lovely wife.

She is equally amazing in the way she handled this adversity. Judy and I actually met Deanna years before we ever met Clebe when she sang at our church in Charleston, South Carolina. Deanna, in addition to having a good singing voice, is a former Miss South Carolina.

The Vietnam War produced some sad accounts, but the most heart-breaking situations occurred when wives of wounded veterans chose to abandon their men. They simply chose not to deal with their wounded husbands and all of the accompanying challenges.

Not Deanna McClary. She is made of durable stuff. Leaving Clebe never crossed her mind. During the days, months, and even years of Clebe's recovery, she stuck by his side. They are still together today, the proud parents of two lovely daughters named Christa and Tara. They live on Pawley's Island and continue to work together in ministry.

Back to Clebe. Formerly a handsome, talented athlete at Clemson, 1Lt. McClary's world had literally been torn apart. For his actions, he earned the Silver Star and Purple Heart. But what about his future? What would he do now? He was missing his left arm, missing his left eye, and left with serious wounds all over the rest of his body. He was told he would never walk again.

Positive Impacts

Remember what I said earlier? We usually can't stop the trials from happening in our lives, but we do get to choose how we respond. And respond Clebe did, and in the most courageous fashion.

On July 26, 1968, Clebe and Deanna attended an evangelistic crusade in Florence, South Carolina, that would change their lives forever. After listening to the evangelist speak, they responded to the altar call and committed their lives to Jesus Christ. Both had been in church many times but had never heard a clear presentation of the gospel. But they each knew there was more. On this night it became personal. Both entered into a personal relationship with God through His Son, Jesus Christ.

It didn't happen overnight, but God worked on Clebe's heart and called him into full-time ministry. The rest is history.

By the time I met Clebe in 1985, he had ministered to tens of thousands. By now it's safe to say that number has grown to hundreds of thousands, if not millions. He has spoken in all 50 states and in 30 countries throughout the world. Still an amazing athlete, Clebe continued to run, participating in many marathons and Special Olympics.

The list of awards and special recognitions Clebe has received is lengthy. Just google his name to find out much more about the things he and Deanna have accomplished since that fateful night on Hill 146 in South Vietnam.

Has adversity knocked you to the mat? Have you gotten up yet? If you have, super! If not, let me assure you that you can — with God's help, of course.

You're thinking: "Scott, you have no idea how tough my situation is and how hopeless I feel. I just can't. I'm destined to a life of simply trying to survive — that's all, nothing more."

Really? Is that what some person has led you to think? Or maybe Satan has deceived you into thinking that your life is all but over, and worth very little.

I don't know you, but whatever dismal report you've heard didn't come from the Lord. Jesus came that you might have life and have it to the full (John 10:10). As long as you have breath in you, God hasn't finished with you. You have purpose and meaning.

The trial, adversity, or whatever has you down isn't enough to stop you — not if you turn to God for help. That's what Clebe did. That's what Deanna did. And that's what millions of others on the planet are doing as well.

"Easy to do?"

"No."

"Will things turn around quickly?"

"Probably not."

"Will it turn out like I want it to?"

"I don't know. God is in charge of the results. You are in charge of trying."

"When should I start?"

"How about now?"

You've heard it before, or certainly something similar: "The journey of a thousand miles begins with a single step." Take that step today. God will help you. And so will others. But you must decide to try. You must take the first step.

A great first step would be to talk to the Lord and ask for His guidance and help. I will even suggest some words to pray. But let me get back to Clebe one more time with a couple of things you might be interested to learn.

By 1985, Clebe had received national attention as a preacher of the gospel and a great motivational speaker in secular settings as well. But he still had challenges. Tough challenges that he had to deal with daily, and still does.

The first morning I met Clebe in 1985, I went to pick him up at the guest quarters on Fort Bragg. He met me at the door of his room, looking very sharp in his Marine combat uniform. But as we shut his door to walk to my car, he looked at me and asked if I would do him a favor.

He needed me to tie his jungle boots. You see, he only had one arm as it was, and even the fingers on his one arm were severely "jacked up." He could speak to thousands, but physically he couldn't tie his bootlaces.

Later on that morning, we were at the mess hall eating breakfast. My commander and some senior non-commissioned officers were spellbound listening to Clebe. But at one point during our breakfast, Clebe leaned over to me and whispered in my ear, "Scott, would you please cut my pancakes?"

Again, 1Lt. McClary's wounds from Vietnam left him unable to perform a simple action like cutting his own pancakes. The lesson is simple. We all have our challenges, some of which will remain with us for a lifetime. But that doesn't mean we can't accomplish the unique mission God assigns to each of us.

Back to the verses I chose to use for this writing — Romans 5:3–4. On the first morning I ever met Clebe, he spoke from this text. They have been indelibly marked in my brain and on my heart since that time:

"Not only so, but we also rejoice in our sufferings, because we know that suffering produces perseverance; perseverance, character; and character, hope."

Positive Impacts

I close with a prayer. I invite you to pray with me:

Lord Jesus, thank You for the truth of verses 3 and 4, that suffering can produce perseverance in my life. And perseverance can develop my character. And as my character grows, I will have hope.

God, I need hope to overcome the adversity in my life. Just as You helped Clebe, help me to get up off the mat and fight the good fight of faith. Help me to know and to accomplish Your will for my life. I want to do this, Jesus. I just need Your help. In Your name, I pray. Amen.

Time now for action. Step up to the next level. And the God of this universe will help you. ■

Stress Improves Performance

Reaching into his bag and taking out a stone, he slung it and struck the Philistine on the forehead. The stone sank into his forehead, and he fell facedown on the ground.
(1 Samuel 17:49)

Stress can improve performance. Can you recall experiences when you did something well beyond your normal capabilities? The pressure was on, and you delivered!

God has engineered us to grow through stressful situations. A great example in the Old Testament is the story of David and Goliath. Picture the scene. A fight to death between the shepherd boy, David, and the Philistine giant, Goliath, was soon to decide the outcome of the battle between Israel and Philistia.

David was approximately 5½ feet tall. Goliath stood over 9 feet. Physically it was no match. But little David was up to the challenge. With a slingshot and one stone, he scored a knock out, killing Goliath and securing victory for Israel. History records that David went on to be a great warrior, poet, musician, and king over Israel.

Facing stressful circumstances, even life-threatening ones? Call on God and let Him help you. Do your part and God will do His. ■

Stress Helps Us to Trust God

Indeed, we felt we had received the sentence of death. But this happened that we might not rely on ourselves but on God, who raises the dead.
(2 Corinthians 1:9)

Warriors routinely encounter difficult situations, some of them life-threatening. Through training and experience, they grow in their ability to survive the most difficult circumstances.

In most respects this is good. Since 9/11, we have developed a military force that is unmatched at anytime in our history.

But training and experience can also create a false sense of confidence in our own abilities. This verse represents an admission by the veteran missionary, Paul, that the hardships he faced nearly killed him.

But Paul quickly points out a positive outcome: He was forced to rely on the Lord more.

Have you ever felt overwhelmed, maybe even on the verge of death? Follow Paul's example. He learned to call on God to rescue him.

Facing a difficult situation? Don't rely solely on your abilities and experience. Cry out to the Lord. He will hear you and provide the support you need. ■

Stress Strengthens the Team

But after the disciples had gathered around him, he got up and went back into the city. The next day he and Barnabas left for Derbe.
(Acts 14:20)

The team that responds best to stress usually wins. We see in it sports, we see it in business, and we see it in the military.

This is also true in the spiritual realm. Luke described a violent scene in the Book of Acts. Paul and some of his missionary team were traveling through ancient Turkey. Paradoxically, because God had used Paul to do a miraculous healing, opposition to the gospel message grew more fierce. Jews from nearby Antioch and Iconium stirred the people of Lystra to kill Paul. They took the apostle to the edge of the city and stoned him, leaving him for dead.

What a blow to this missionary team. But instead of stressing out, they rose to the occasion. Calling upon the power of God, these men gathered around Paul and prayed. Soon the veteran missionary was back on his feet.

Then another amazing thing happened. Instead of fleeing, Paul and his team went right back into the city.

Stress had strengthened the team. ■

Stress Maximizes Our Coping Abilities

But Eleazar stood his ground and struck down the Philistines till his hand grew tired and froze to the sword. The LORD brought about a great victory that day. The troops returned to Eleazar, but only to strip the dead.
(2 Samuel 23:10)

It's simply true. When danger is imminent, most people vote for self-preservation. They run, they duck, they flee for safety.

But there are exceptions. True leaders respond to stressful conditions and take the necessary steps to deal with the situation.

Eleazar was a leader who chose not to run from almost certain death. Rather, he decided to stand and fight against a fierce enemy while the rest of the Israelite army sounded retreat and fled. History records that God used Eleazar's magnificent efforts to win a great victory for Israel that day. Small wonder that the Bible labels Eleazar as one of David's "mighty men."

It seems reasonable to say that Eleazar may have never known how great a warrior he was without this test. He could have run, but he didn't.

Are you facing stressful, adverse conditions? Perhaps they are even life-threatening. Like Eleazar, don't run. Stand fast. Trust God. He will give you victory. ■

Suffering Produces Perseverance

*Not only so, but we also glory in our sufferings,
because we know that suffering produces
perseverance.*
(Romans 5:3)

Perseverance is an essential quality for success in life. This is especially true for those serving in the profession of arms.

Select any area of life — work, sports, finances, health, parenting, etc. Rarely does success come without perseverance. Though we love to hear the great accomplishments of those who chose to persevere, developing the quality of perseverance doesn't come without cost.

So how do we get perseverance? As the verse above tells us, often it comes through suffering.

Military life brings suffering on many fronts. Warriors engaged in combat certainly experience suffering, especially those who are wounded. But warriors are not the only ones. Family members, especially those whose loved ones have been killed or wounded, live with untold pain. And then there is separation due to deployment. You get the point. There is plenty of suffering to go around.

Going through a time of personal suffering? Take heart. Suffering produces perseverance, and perseverance will help you succeed in life. ∎

Perseverance Develops Character

*Not only so, but we also rejoice in our sufferings,
because we know that suffering produces
perseverance; perseverance, character;
and character, hope.
(Romans 5:3–4)*

Hardships in life provide opportunities to develop our character. But it's not automatic. We must choose to grow. And growth can be painful.

In the previous devotion, we learned that suffering produces perseverance. Taking this a step further, verse 4 tells us that perseverance produces character.

I like the way Abraham Lincoln put it: "Character is like a tree and reputation like its shadow. The shadow is what we think of it; the tree is the real thing."

Years ago, I had a conversation with a command sergeant major that gave me a glimpse into his character development. As a young private, he felt he could never live up to his squad leader's expectations. His sergeant was always on his back. Finally one day, the private made a decision. Enough is enough.

He went to his squad leader and said, "Sergeant, if you can dish it out, I can take it!"

That's character! ■

Stress Helps Us to Be Humble

*In order to keep me from becoming conceited,
I was given a thorn in my flesh, a messenger of Satan,
to torment me.*
(2 Corinthians 12:7)

Humility is a character trait many claim to want. But have you noticed how difficult it is to become genuinely humble? Not easy!

Stressful circumstances can actually help us with humility. The apostle Paul was given amazing revelations by God, even to include a glimpse of heaven. But as this verse tells us, the Lord allowed a stressor to keep Paul humble. Paul was given a thorn in the flesh. It may have been a physical problem. Bible scholars offer differing opinions, but we don't know for sure. In any case, Paul admits that the thorn certainly helped him from becoming conceited.

Recently I watched some high school all-star basketball players perform on national television. A few stood out as "show offs" and were obviously impressed with themselves. Just wait until their first days with a good college or NBA team. They will most likely be humbled quickly!

Stress isn't always negative. It can help to keep us humble. And that's a good thing. ∎

I Am in Desperate Need

Listen to my cry, for I am in desperate need;
rescue me from those who pursue me,
for they are too strong for me.
(Psalm 142:6)

I have learned two key truths about connecting with God. They both pertain to God himself. First, He desires a relationship with each one of us, but He will not override our free will. He doesn't force us into a relationship.

Second, though the Lord has the answers and resources for any need we could ever have, we must ask. We have to take the initiative and petition Him for help.

Think about it — it's difficult to help someone who won't admit to having needs or who will not ask for help. All too frequently, this describes the situation our nation faces in attempting to help many of our military veterans.

Much of the challenge exists because of the ethos within the military. Ethos has its derivation from a Latin word meaning customs. In present-day usage, ethos is the spirit that characterizes a particular culture or organization. Given the protracted wars in Iraq and Afghanistan, we presently describe our military as having a warrior ethos. This is unquestionably true, but there are pros and cons. Among the cons are several factors that make warriors hesitant to ask for help.

Let me illustrate with a couple of examples. While serving as an infantry company commander in the mid-70s, I once directed that all E-6 and above personnel in the unit fill out a questionnaire. It was a simple drill that required taking a 3 x 5 card and listing answers to two questions. On one side of the card, I requested that they list their strengths. On the other side, I wanted them to list their weaknesses. I then met with every non-commissioned officer (NCO) and officer to discuss their responses.

I vividly recall my discussion with one NCO. He came into my office, handed me his card, and sat quietly until I had reviewed his information. On the side listing strengths, he had written somewhere between 10 and 15 items. I looked them over and agreed that he had many strong areas.

When I turned the card over, it was blank. My conversation with him went something like this: "SSG Jones (not his real name), did you forget to list your weaknesses?"

SSG Jones: "No, sir. I really don't think I have any."

I then replied, "Well, I can think of one for a starter. Either you are incredibly arrogant, or you have blind spots that prevent you from being objective about yourself."

This outstanding NCO looked stunned by my comment, but then began to open up to me. We had an amazing conversation during which he admitted to having a number of areas that needed improvement. We discussed his strengths and weaknesses for a few minutes, and I closed our session by affirming his strengths, performance, and potential.

Was SSG Jones simply arrogant about his strengths and blind to his shortcomings? Perhaps a little of each, but more likely he desperately wanted to reflect his understanding of the warrior ethos as he spoke to his commander. In his mind, the warrior ethos meant "no weakness."

Another reason warriors won't ask for help relates to perception. Consider Post Traumatic Stress (PTS) and Post Traumatic Stress Disorder (PTSD) — both continue to be tough issues. In many parts of the military, there is a stigma associated with admitting to either or both of these conditions. Since these relate to mental and psychological wounds versus physical wounds, they are viewed as signs of weakness.

So how do many warriors deal with this stigma? They simply will not seek help. They fear being thought of as weak, or in some cases they are afraid that seeing a psychologist or psychiatrist automatically labels them as "head cases" who will be processed out of the military.

There are additional reasons why warriors will not seek God's help. Some simply deny having problems at all. Others believe they will be able to handle the situation on

their own. A few believe they have
done bad things and God is not
interested in helping them. And the
list goes on.

Allow me to state it bluntly: No human being
has it all together. We all have problems, we
all get stressed, and we all need help beyond
ourselves.

God is there for you — always. No problem is
too big or complex.

David was one of the most incredible people
who has ever lived. He was a king, a poet, a
musician, and a warrior. He killed the giant,
Goliath; nations bowed at his feet; his writings
have been read and studied for centuries. But consider the
words he wrote in Psalm 142: "Listen to my cry, for I am
in desperate need; rescue me from those who pursue me,
for they are too strong for me."

David wrote the psalm at a time when he was fighting
for his life and about to be overtaken by his enemies.
His strength and resources couldn't cut it. He saw his
situation for what it really was. He needed divine help.

Think about David and think about your own
situation. Was David a warrior? Absolutely — as good
as they come. But he realized his limitations as a human
being and cried out to God.

Are you a warrior? Certainly — and probably a very good one. But if your circumstances are too much for you to handle alone, why not ask for help? Why not turn to God and cry out to Him?

Do you need help with health issues, a job situation, a relationship problem, an overwhelming fear, depression? Regardless of your need, the Lord can help you.

But it's up to you to ask. ■

Warriors Need to Remember Their Fallen

*Godly men buried Stephen and mourned
deeply for him.
(Acts 8:2)*

Picture the scene at the grave site. Hundreds of Christians had gathered to mourn the loss of a great leader named Stephen. Stephen had courageously held his ground against the religious leaders. But the mock trial ended in his conviction. They stoned Stephen to death.

The death of the first Christian martyr was a huge blow to followers of the Way. Stephen had been a powerful preacher, gifted teacher, and loyal friend. It was not only proper to hold a funeral in Stephen's honor, but it was also very necessary for those remaining behind. The sudden loss of this Spirit-filled man had stunned and saddened them. They needed to take time to honor their fallen comrade and to grieve his passing.

Warriors die — in combat and even during peacetime. Either way, fellow warriors need to honor their fallen and grieve their loss. Funeral services and memorial services are the formal methods, but there are other ways as well. The important point to remember is that every person needs time to grieve during times of loss.

It's not weakness to grieve when you lose fellow warriors. It's right and it's necessary. ■

Warriors Need Forgiveness

Blessed is the one whose transgressions are forgiven, whose sins are covered.
(Psalm 32:1)

Warriors returning home need many things, but none is more important than being at peace with their Maker.

Tears streamed down his face as the soldier related his story. It was a story of violence, confusion, pain, death, and "what-ifs." A fellow soldier had died from the IED (Improvised Explosive Device) blast. The man across from me was agonizing over the "what-ifs." Although the enemy had planted the IED, somehow he felt responsible. In his mind, he should have spotted the bomb; he should have warned the driver. Somehow, according to his thinking, he could have prevented the entire disaster if he had been more alert.

I couldn't legitimately talk the soldier out of feeling guilty. I wasn't there. But I could remind him of our merciful God who forgives and purifies. We prayed. A wonderful calm came over this soldier. He sensed God's forgiveness and he seemed to have new hope and perspective on the event. I could tell that an important need had been met. Not by me, but by the Lord.

As Psalm 32:1 tells us, "Blessed is the one whose transgressions are forgiven." ■

Warriors Need Hope

"For I know the plans I have for you," declares the
LORD, *"plans to prosper you and not to harm you,*
plans to give you hope and a future."
(Jeremiah 29:11)

Every warrior needs hope, especially when times are
tough.

In 1985, I was Chaplain for the 82nd Signal Battalion,
and we were doing a tough PT run. The run was of
unknown distance. The Battalion Commander wanted to
see how mentally tough we were.

About five miles into the run, we entered an area
known as the "clay pits," a wide-open area with a giant
pit about a quarter mile in diameter. As soldiers grew
more tired, the unit stretched out for hundreds of yards as
we circled the perimeter of the pit. Soldiers began to drop
out. Not knowing where the finish line was, many had
psyched themselves out and quit.

But then an amazing thing happened. Soldiers
throughout the formation looked across the clay pits to
the head of the formation. A Marine with one arm was
still running strong. His name was Lt. Clebe McClary.

Inspired by this wounded Vietnam veteran, warriors
now ran with hope. And that is God's plan for you —
hope and a future. ■

Warriors Need to Tell Their Story

He replied, "I have been very zealous for the LORD God Almighty. The Israelites have rejected your covenant, torn down your altars, and put your prophets to death with the sword. I am the only one left, and now they are trying to kill me too."
(1 Kings 19:10)

Everyone has a story — a story that needs to be told. This especially applies to warriors who have experienced the trauma of war.

Take the Old Testament prophet, Elijah. In this verse, he is telling God his story. Just days prior he had a showdown with 450 priests of Baal. Elijah had won the contest and subsequently ordered the death of all of the priests. But now he was running for his life. Queen Jezebel was seeking revenge and would surely kill Elijah if she could catch him.

The Lord listened to what Elijah needed.

Two good teaching points emerge from this story. First, if you are a warrior who has experienced trauma, tell your story. Tell it to God, another person, or both. It will help.

Second, if you are trying to support a returning warrior, be a good listener. It will help more than you know. ◼

Warriors Need to Know They Are Loved

"For God so loved the world that he gave his one and only Son, that whoever believes in him shall not perish but have eternal life."
(John 3:16)

His troops said he was a hard man — hard as woodpecker lips. But he needed to know he was loved. From all appearances, he was dying.

As this career non-commissioned officer lay on his hospital bed, I looked at him and said, "I know you want straight talk. Have you made peace with God?"

"Chaplain, no, I haven't. How could I? I have done too many bad things."

"First Sergeant, you are not wrong about much, but you are way off on this one. God loves you unconditionally, regardless of what you have done."

I could tell I had his attention. I read John 3:16 and said, "You see — God loves you. Will you place your faith in Him?"

"Chaplain, I'm not long for this world. I would like to do that."

I led him in prayer to receive Jesus as his Savior. He died less than 48 hours later. This warrior knew he was loved. He knew he had peace with God. ∎

Warriors Make a Difference

But Shammah took his stand in the middle of the field. He defended it and struck the Philistines down, and the LORD brought about a great victory.
(2 Samuel 23:12)

God has created every person on the planet for a purpose. Warriors are certainly no exception. And like all other people, warriors need to know that their lives have made a positive difference. This desire to contribute to those around them is God-given.

Many Vietnam veterans have never received affirmation for their sacrifices during that war. They don't know that their efforts made any difference. Hopefully our present and future warriors will not have to repeat this experience.

Notice the verse from 2 Samuel. The Bible records that Shammah, one of David's mighty men, fought valiantly and helped the Israelites achieve a great victory. Shammah's heroic efforts made an enormous difference.

If you are a veteran, please know that your contributions have helped our nation. Your contributions have been valuable. Thank you.

If you are the spouse, child, parent, or friend of a military person, thanks for supporting your veteran, and thanks for your efforts as well. You, too, have made a positive difference! ■

Warriors Need Time to Reintegrate

*There is a time for everything, and a season for
every activity under heaven: . . . a time to kill
and a time to heal,
(Ecclesiastes 3:1,3)*

Life for the military community moves at a fast
clip, and there are many adjustments. One of the most
challenging adjustments occurs when warriors transition
from the battlefield back to home, often in a few short
days. We call this process "reintegration."

The last several years have demonstrated how difficult
this can be. Despite high expectations of warriors and
families alike, the results have often been heart-breaking:
marital strife that often ends in divorce, domestic
violence, addiction to drugs and alcohol, and financial
problems to name a few.

God's Word has sage advice: Time is the key. "There
is a time for everything," the Scripture tells us. There is a
time for reintegration.

Warriors and families must realize this and be patient
with one another. Warriors have changed, and so have
their spouses and children.

Give yourself time. It's God's way. ∎

Choices

Two Men; Two Choices

Then Peter remembered the word Jesus had spoken: "Before the rooster crows, you will disown me three times." And he went outside and wept bitterly.
(Matthew 26:75)

When Judas, who had betrayed him, saw that Jesus was condemned, he was seized with remorse and returned the thirty silver coins to the chief priests and the elders. "I have sinned," he said, "for I have betrayed innocent blood."

"What is that to us?" they replied. "That's your responsibility."

So Judas threw the money into the temple and left. Then he went away and hanged himself.
(Matthew 27:3–5)

Life offers us choices, and choices matter because they impact others and ourselves.

One important category of choices relates to the decisions we make during times of stress, pressure, and crisis. Typically, people are not at their strongest in these situations. They are not thinking as clearly, don't have their normal perspective, and often let their emotions override sound judgment.

The results of choices range from inconsequential to major, from immediate to long range, from temporary to eternal. But the bottom line is simple: Good decisions are better than poor ones.

I recall a young lady at one military installation who came to see me. She had entered into a relationship with a young officer on post and made a poor decision that resulted in her becoming pregnant. But that was hardly the end of her stress. Although marriage was out of the question, the officer voluntarily offered child support once the baby was born. However, he changed his mind. He was not going to help her financially and now encouraged her to terminate her pregnancy.

The young lady's world had been turned upside down, but she didn't lose her head. I encouraged her not to terminate her pregnancy and helped her explore options once the baby was born. She prayed to the Lord for wisdom and guidance. She made the choice to have the baby. In the months following the birth of her daughter, she came to see me a couple of times. She thanked me many times for my assistance, particularly my encouragement to her to seek God's guidance in the whole matter. She beamed with joy and happiness. Though she had made one poor decision that created great stress in her life, she responded in a godly manner. She made the right choice.

Making sound decisions during challenging times is not easy, nor is it automatic. The ability to decide wisely doesn't necessarily correlate to a person's age, experience, education, or financial status. All of these can factor significantly into our ability to make wise choices, but they are not determinate.

We always need God's help, but particularly during times in our lives when stressful conditions seem overwhelming to us. We need to know that God cares, that He understands, and that He loves us unconditionally. We also want assurance that God has the clout to help us — that nothing is too difficult for Him.

Sometimes, our circumstances may appear so dark that we don't even know how we will keep going. Hopelessness, depression, lack of purpose — God is able to deal with any of these issues, and much more.

Perhaps above anything else that the Lord provides for us, we need His wisdom. The good news is that God's wisdom is available. The Bible tells us this is James 1:5: "If any of you lacks wisdom, you should ask God, who gives generously to all without finding fault, and it will be given to you."

The bad news, however, is that in desperate circumstances many people don't seek it. They go after information from other sources and often wind up making the wrong choice.

There is one vital reality regarding the choices we make, and many still haven't accepted the truth on this one. Regardless of the situation and how hard it may be, the individual has to assume responsibility for the choice. Yes, there can be huge pressure from many sides, but ultimately we make the decision, not someone else.

Why is this so crucial? Because if we continually blame the circumstances, another person, or cite something else as the reason for the choice, we never learn to take the responsibility for our own actions. We don't learn to seek the truth and deal squarely with the facts. We never develop our God-given potential as human beings to behave in ways that honor God.

In the final analysis, God will judge each of us for the things we have done or left undone. It makes a lot more sense to understand this now and start accepting responsibility for our choices. God is just and fair. But the Bible makes it clear that He will hold each of us accountable for our decisions.

By this point, I trust you are more persuaded to seek the Lord during your trials. Even if you are the culprit and brought the circumstances upon yourself, our gracious God is available to help. But the choice to seek His support belongs to you.

Let's conclude this discussion about choices by contrasting two biblical figures. Each encountered an incredibly tough set of circumstances. Each had to make

a choice. As we examine their situations along with
the decisions each made, note the stark contrast in the
consequences of their choices.

The two men are Peter and Judas, both among Jesus'
original 12 disciples. Both men were part of the select
group that traveled with Jesus during His 3 years of
ministry. Both were recipients of His teaching and
witnessed the many miracles Jesus did. Both were present
with Jesus in the upper room when the Master shared one
final meal with His followers. During the time of Jesus
arrest and mock trial, both found themselves in the most
stressful circumstances of their lives.

Consider Judas, the disciple whose betrayal
prompted the religious leaders to arrest Jesus. After
a long night of inquisition, Jesus received the death
sentence. Scripture tells us that at this point Judas
realized his wrongdoing and went back to the religious
leaders to confess his sin. Despite Judas' admission, the
decision to kill Jesus still stood.

It's impossible to put ourselves in the shoes of the very
man who betrayed Jesus Christ. But we can examine the
breath of Scripture and conclude that Judas' decision to
take his own life was not his only choice. His was a tragic
decision with eternal consequences. Nothing in the Bible
provides evidence that Judas made heaven. The evidence
seems to indicate just the opposite — that Judas will
spend eternity separated from God.

A bad choice under unimaginably stressful conditions. Could Judas have sought God for forgiveness? Could he have reset the course of his life and continued serving as a disciple of Christ? The answer is a resounding, "Yes." But that's not the choice Judas made. He decided to take his own life, and he bears full responsibility for it.

Let's review Peter's situation. Leading up to his arrest, Jesus had told Peter that the disciple would deny Him three times. Unquestionably, Peter didn't believe it. But following Jesus' arrest, things started to unravel for the brash disciple. On three separate occasions, Peter denied ever having been with Jesus. Following his last denial, the rooster crowed just as Jesus had foretold.

Peter was both stunned and shocked by his lack of courage. All of his claims about remaining loyal to Jesus, even to his own death, were apparently nothing but hot air. During the most crucial moments to date, Peter had failed his Lord. What could have been worse?

Like Judas in many respects, Peter had failed Jesus. But unlike Judas, Peter exercised a radically different choice. Instead of deciding to take his own life, he doubtlessly sought forgiveness and direction from God through prayer. Only Peter and God alone could know how painful the next few days must have been. Jesus, their leader, gets crucified and buried.

Peter, along with the other followers, had no idea what was coming next. News of the Resurrection must have amazed Peter, but not nearly as much as the appearances Jesus made to the disciples following His rising from the dead.

The most special occurred when Jesus appeared to Peter and a few of the disciples along the shore of the Sea of Galilee. At that time, the Gospel of John records a conversation between Jesus and Peter. The essence of the discussion focused around Jesus telling Peter to continue his ministry. Phrases like "feed my sheep" and "follow me" gave new meaning and purpose to Peter's life.

The rest is history. Peter went on to become the recognized leader of the disciples. He even wrote two books of the Bible — 1 and 2 Peter. Until his death, Peter's life was totally committed to preaching the gospel and building the Church. Though not fully substantiated, Christian tradition reports that Peter died a martyr's death by being crucified upside down. The upside-down part was at Peter's own request, for he didn't feel worthy to be crucified in the same manner as his Lord.

Two men. Two choices.

Seek God. Make the right choices. ■

Turn to God for Help

> *"Our God, will you not judge them?*
> *For we have no power to face this vast army*
> *that is attacking us. We do not know what to do,*
> *but our eyes are on you."*
> *(2 Chronicles 20:12)*

The Lord wants us to ask for His help — in the good times and the bad.

Strangely, however, people frequently don't turn to God in times of need. Why? For many, it's simply pride. They think they can handle the situation themselves. A few don't believe they are worthy of God's help — so they don't ask. Still others seek worldly sources of support and don't bother to ask the Lord.

The Bible couldn't be more clear. God cares, He has the power and resources to help, and He wants us to ask Him.

In this verse from 2 Chronicles, Jehoshaphat, king of Judah, had the good sense to ask God for help against an overwhelming enemy force. Militarily, the Israelites were no match. God heard and answered his prayers. They were victorious with God's help!

What about you? Are you facing circumstances beyond your human capabilities? Follow Jehoshaphat's example and ask God to help you. ■

Seek Forgiveness Now

Jesus answered him, "Truly I tell you, today you will be with me in paradise."
(Luke 23:43)

War requires its participants to do some hard things, especially in the taking of human life. It's not unusual for warriors to carry feelings of guilt and shame for long periods, even to their grave. This is not God's intent. He offers forgiveness and comfort for anyone who will seek Him with a sincere heart.

Consider the situation at Golgotha on the day Jesus died. He was crucified with two criminals; one on His right, the other on His left. One criminal hurled insults at Jesus. But the other petitioned Him: "Jesus, remember me when you come into your kingdom." Implied with his statement was the criminal's request for forgiveness for his sins.

Note Jesus' response in today's verse. He forgave the criminal and assured the man that heaven awaited him. The request came just in time, only hours before the criminal's death.

But why should you and I wait? If you are wrestling with guilt, shame, or any other problem, simply make your request to Jesus.

No situation is beyond God's ability to forgive or comfort. Seek forgiveness NOW. ∎

Keep a Positive Outlook

The LORD will vindicate me; your love, LORD, endures forever — do not abandon the works of your hands.
(Psalm 138:8)

King David experienced many times of trial and heartache, but he consistently chose to maintain a positive outlook.

In verse 7 of Psalm 138, David candidly admits to having tough challenges: "Though I walk in the midst of trouble, you preserve my life." David's life included violence, bloodshed, betrayal, murder, domestic problems, and much more. But he refused to give in to Satan's efforts to take him down spiritually, mentally, emotionally, or physically. Rather, he chose to trust the Lord.

What about you? Undoubtedly you've had trials and adversity of your own, and almost certainly to the point of feeling discouraged, depressed, and alone — or even worse. At those times, did you try to operate in your own strength? You probably discovered this approach rarely works. The Lord didn't create us to go it alone.

Follow David's example and trust God. The Lord strengthened his faith and gave him hope. During hard times, David knew God wouldn't abandon him, but would fulfill His purpose for David's life.

And God will fulfill His purpose for your life. ■

Don't Isolate Yourself

Then Joab went into the house to the king and said, "Today you have humiliated all your men, who have just saved your life and the lives of your sons and daughters and the lives of your wives and concubines."
(2 Samuel 19:5)

When personal crisis happens, many people seek isolation. Rather than sharing their trauma and pain with others, they prefer to be alone. Warriors sometimes make this choice, but usually it's not a good one.

Why? For one, it is difficult to maintain proper perspective during difficult situations. Being alone eliminates the wisdom and support that others can provide. Additionally, aloneness tends to open one's mind to negative self-talk.

Take King David. Receiving news that his son, Absalom, had been killed, David went into isolation to mourn. Understandable — to a point. But David went overboard. While focused on his own grief, he lost perspective regarding his leadership responsibilities.

Finally, one of his army generals named Joab confronted David. David had seemingly forgotten his many followers who had risked their lives to save him. In short, he humiliated them.

Experiencing traumatic times? Don't isolate yourself. Seek help from others. ∎

Believe God's Report About You

*"Why did I not perish at birth, and die as
I came from the womb?"*
(Job 3:11)

Have you ever experienced something so painful
or so horrific that you questioned why you were even
alive?

Actually, most of us feel this way at some time in our
lives: the Marine who has lost all of his limbs from an
IED (Improvised Explosive Device) explosion; the wife
whose warrior recently died in combat; the middle-
aged man who has just received word that his cancer is
terminal.

Even Job, a righteous man in the Old Testament, lost
sight that his life had meaning and purpose. He had
lost his children, his wealth, and his health. Physically,
he was in agony; emotionally, he was in despair;
spiritually, he felt bankrupt. In short, he wanted to die.

But then he heard God's report. His life did have
meaning and the Lord was working His purposes in
Job's life, even through suffering.

Regardless of how hopeless your life may seem at
present, you have purpose and meaning. Your Creator
says so. Believe God's report! ∎

Don't Turn to Cheap Substitutes

They shed innocent blood, the blood of their sons and daughters, whom they sacrificed to the idols of Canaan, and the land was desecrated by their blood.
(Psalm 106:38)

Stress from trauma and crisis can warp our perspective and tempt good people to turn to wrong places for answers. The results can be disastrous.

This verse refers to a time when the people of Israel foolishly turned from God and pursued the false gods of Canaan. In their deception, Israelite parents actually sacrificed their children to idols. How tragic!

Today, too many members of the military community are turning to the wrong places for solutions to their problems. Drugs and alcohol are not the right answers for the pain of PTS, PTSD, or any other problems.

A few years ago a young woman came to see me. She was pregnant out of wedlock. Abortion seemed attractive because the problem would just go away. But would it? We talked about other women who had gone this route and how much they regretted taking the life of an unborn child. We also looked at counsel from God's Word.

She chose life for her child. Cheap substitutes don't work. ■

Don't Ever Quit!

*When he heard that it was Jesus of Nazareth, he
began to shout, "Jesus, Son of David,
have mercy on me!"
(Mark 10:47)*

Life can get hard at times — so hard that you feel like
quitting. Don't! God has things for you to do.

Bartimaeus undoubtedly experienced many days when
he felt like giving up. After all, he was a beggar and he
was blind. A good day for him was receiving enough
coins in his cup to buy food for the day. Life for him
seemed hopeless — begging, eating, and sleeping.

Hopelessness changed to hope the day Bartimaeus
met Jesus. As Jesus was walking past him, Bartimaeus
shouted at the top of his lungs: "Jesus, Son of David,
have mercy on me!"

Despite Jesus' disciples trying to quiet him,
Bartimaeus would not quit shouting. Jesus heard him
and called for him. Jesus performed a miracle that day
by restoring Bartimaeus' sight. Bartimaeus would never
be the same. He had been touched by the Master.

Is your life really tough these days, even to the point
of feeling like you want to quit?

Don't! All you need is the touch of the Master. Cry
out to Him today! ∎

Who Are You, Lord?

*We all fell to the ground, and I heard a voice
saying to me in Aramaic, "Saul, Saul, why do you
persecute me? It is hard for you to kick against the
goads." Then I asked, "Who are you, Lord?"
(Acts 26:14-15)*

Our Creator has made each one of us for a purpose.
It is our responsibility to discover that purpose and
fulfill it.

The storms of life can cause serious damage, but
they can also motivate us to sharpen our focus, find
our purpose, and accomplish it. By now, in reading
this devotional book, I trust you are starting to be
convinced that stress is not all bad. Nor is trauma or
crisis. Suffering, by God's design, is one of His most
useful tools. But we have to believe that and respond in
the right way.

Though I don't know you personally, nor am I
familiar with your life or present circumstances, I
believe God has designed an amazing future for you.
You may be a young sailor, a WWII veteran, a military
brat, or a civilian working for the Department of
Defense — God's plans for you are good plans, plans
with hope and a future.

My statement requires one qualification: I'm talking
about God's plans, not your plans or my plans. It's quite
conceivable that they are one and the same. If that's

true, wonderful! If not, we must continue to engage in serving God and trying to discover or rediscover what God wants us to do.

This devotional book has focused on dealing with stress and hard times. Is it possible to discover God's plan and purpose for our lives during times of turbulence and even chaos? Wouldn't it be better if we let things calm down and take this thing much more slowly?

Maybe, but often it doesn't work that way. More frequently, God uses periods of crisis and confusion to get our attention, sort some things out, and get on the path of doing God's will. We usually don't figure this out on our own. The Lord knows this and provides a divine shove to move us in the right direction. And He does this in His perfect timing, not ours.

The verses at the beginning of this story refer to Paul, the great missionary whom God chose to take the gospel message beyond Israel to the rest of the world. At the time of this incident, Paul was still called Saul. Verse 15 records the question Saul asked God on the day that the Lord decided to rock his world. The question? "Who are you, Lord?"

You see, at the time Saul asked this question, he thought he was on a mission for God, a mission designed to stamp out a cult whose leader was Jesus. The members of this group were spreading all sorts of religious lies and heresies that opposed the teaching of the top Jewish leaders. Saul was on his way to Damascus in Syria to arrest a few more of these zealots before they got out of control.

Only one problem: Saul didn't have a clue as to what he was really doing. So God decided to give him a shove. As Saul neared Damascus, a bright light appeared, so bright that it knocked Saul to the ground. Then a voice spoke to him, "Saul, Saul, why do you persecute me?"

At this point, Saul asked his question: "Who are you, Lord?"

The answer was not what Saul expected. "I am Jesus, whom you are persecuting."

But Jesus wasn't finished speaking. He issued Saul some new marching orders:

"Now get up and go into the city, and you will be told what you must do."
(Acts 9:6)

No explanation from Jesus. No big picture overview to provide Saul with context for the situation. Just go to Damascus and await further instructions. And did I mention that Saul was now blind? A great start to his new ministry.

Confusion, bewilderment, disorientation — all the stress you could possibly imagine. Not to mention that Saul suddenly realized that his service for God had been routed in the wrong direction. Quite a revelation.

Saul obeyed the Lord. His world turned upside down, inside out. But now he was headed in the direction of God's will. In the near future his name would change to Paul, and he would become a great leader of the newly birthed Christian faith. The Lord would choose Paul to author approximately 25 percent of the New Testament.

It took getting into Paul's personal space and shaking him to his very foundation. And throughout the remainder of his life and ministry, it required the Lord's encouragement and guidance because the Lord had purposed some extremely difficult missions for him to do. To the natural eye, Paul's life didn't end well — beheaded in a Roman prison. In God's sight, though, Paul brought glory to God. He fought the good fight and finished well.

Finishing well? Isn't that what we all want to do? To know that we have lived a life that has served God and man, and really counted for something. The truth is that any of us can do this. It is absolutely what the Lord wants for your life.

Future Possibilities

So get ready! Your future begins now. It will be exciting and loaded with good things — satisfying and useful things that will bring contentment to your soul.

But don't misunderstand. There will likely be stress, and plenty of it. There will be dark times, hard situations, and moments of confusion and doubt. It all comes with the package deal of selling ourselves out to Jesus.

It's a deal you can take or leave. I highly recommend you take it and run with every ounce of energy and commitment you can muster. God will run with you, from now and throughout eternity. ■

It's Not Over Till It's Over

*The LORD blessed the latter part of Job's life more
than the former part. He had fourteen thousand
sheep, six thousand camels, a thousand yoke of
oxen and a thousand donkeys. And he also had
seven sons and three daughters.*
(Job 42:12–13)

Yogi Berra, Hall of Fame catcher for the New York
Yankees, is credited with the phrase, "It's not over till
it's over." No matter the odds of winning the game, the
outcome is not decided until the game is over.

This is true about life regardless of how dark or
dismal things presently appear. God has the final vote.
Consider Job, a Bible figure who lived thousands of
years ago. Through a tragic series of events, Job lost his
children, his wealth, and his health. It got so bad that
Job's wife told him to curse God and die.

But Job clung to his faith. In the end, God blessed
him more than He had previously. The Lord gave him
beautiful children, incredible wealth, and health that
allowed him to live 140 years.

Have stressful events left you feeling liked "damaged
goods"? Hold on to your faith. God is not finished with
you yet! ∎

Fellow Warriors Will Help You

But after the disciples had gathered around him,
he got up and went back into the city. The next day
he and Barnabas left for Derbe.
(Acts 14:20)

UFC (Ultimate Fighter Championship) is a fast-growing sport that brings together the world's toughest mixed martial artists. But know what? None of them are invincible, and eventually every one of them gets knocked down or even knocked out.

Take note: After getting knocked down, they get back up. Maybe not in that fight, or even over the next few days. But they do get up and fight again.

Prolonged war in Iraq and Afghanistan has taken its toll on warriors and families. Warriors have taken hits, and so have families. It's nothing to be ashamed or embarrassed about. The key is to get back up.

The apostle Paul was stoned and left for dead. But his disciples surrounded him and helped him to his feet to continue his mission.

Have you been knocked down? Everyone experiences that at some point. But you can get back up. Fellow warriors, friends, and family are waiting to help you. And so is God.

Your best days lie ahead — not behind. ∎

God Never Wastes an Experience

Now I want you to know, brothers and sisters, that what has happened to me has actually served to advance the gospel.
(Philippians 1:12)

Have you noticed that the really difficult times in your life have turned out to be beneficial?

God knows this, even while we are still going through these times. He allows these experiences because He knows there will be future benefits — for you and maybe for others.

Paul was in a Roman jail, even though he had committed no crime. But he soon realized that his suffering also brought opportunity. He was now able to share his faith in the most powerful city in the world.

A good friend of mine, a military chaplain, was suffering from PTSD a few years ago. He showed the courage to tell his chain of command. The news was not well-received. The military discharged him a number of months later for health reasons.

But guess what? His boldness paved the way for others suffering from PTSD. The military has since made great strides in treating this disorder.

And my friend? He's doing valuable ministry and helping many. God never wastes an experience! ∎

Make Every Day Count

"For I know the plans I have for you," declares the
LORD, *"plans to prosper you and not to harm you,*
plans to give you hope and a future."
(Jeremiah 29:11)

Your plans, your hopes, and your dreams are very important to God.

So how can we make every day count? It begins by realizing that God has created each and every day — for you and for me. We can choose to be glad. We can choose to rejoice. It's our decision.

Admittedly, during our down times, this is hard to do. Many warriors and families have endured really tough things. They are thinking more about surviving than thriving.

I recently heard about a young warrior in an EOD Unit (Explosive Ordinance Detachment) who suffered terrible burns from an IED (Improvised Explosive Device). The doctors wanted to take a huge skin graft from his chest. The soldier refused, saying to take it from his "back side." The medical folks warned that healing would be much more painful.

The soldier responded: "Next summer I will be mowing my grass with my shirt off. I want my chest to look good!"

Better days are coming! ■

Your Plans Will Succeed

Commit to the LORD whatever you do, and he will establish your plans.
(Proverbs 16:3)

Success is contagious. We draw encouragement from others who have overcome adversity and done great things.

Perhaps you're struggling at present and need to experience a few successes in your life. You can!

So let's get started. First, check with God about your plans. Are your plans in line with His will? As you pray, He will show you. Assuming you have a green light, commit your plans to Him and act on His promise. He says that when you commit your plans to Him, they will succeed.

A few years ago, I met a young man who dreamed about becoming a Navy SEAL. I put him in touch with a Navy SEAL as a means of encouraging him. Just this past summer, the young man came to see me and told me he was applying to the United States Naval Academy. He still plans to become a SEAL.

While I don't know his future, I predict he will succeed. Why? Because I know this young man has committed his plans to God and is taking action on God's promise.

You can do the same! ∎

Replacing the Old With the New

Therefore, if anyone is in Christ, the new creation has come: The old has gone, the new is here!
(2 Corinthians 5:17)

There is a saying that makes a lot of sense: "More of the same never brings change." Many never change because they're not open to anything new.

I remember him well. He was competent in his job, but was also one of the meanest and most crusty people I had ever met. He was an Army master sergeant at Fort Bragg. Working with him was not enjoyable, especially since I was a young infantry lieutenant with no experience.

Years later I was back at Bragg, but this time as a chaplain. One day this former master sergeant showed up in the unit area. Same looks on the outside, but what a different person! He exuded excitement about life. He was kind and very interested in other people.

I had to find out how this happened. He shared with me that he had invited Christ into his life, and the changes began. New attitudes replaced old ones. He had become a new person.

If you haven't already, consider inviting the Lord into your life today. ∎

Well Done!

*His master replied, "Well done, good and faithful
servant! You have been faithful with a few things;
I will put you in charge of many things. Come and
share your master's happiness!"
(Matthew 25:23)*

We all need to know that our life counts, particularly
in the work we do. The military does this well through
its system of promotions and awards. Although not
perfect, usually the right people get promoted or
receive awards for their efforts.

The Lord has a system for promotions and rewards
as well, one that can't be messed up by another person.
In the Parable of the Talents, Jesus illustrated the truth
that God has given each of us gifts and abilities, which
He expects us to use to the best of our ability. We
will — or will not —be rewarded accordingly.

No matter how difficult or stressed your life seems,
remember that you alone decide your outcome with the
Lord. If you serve Him to the best of your ability, you
can be certain you will please the Master. In this life,
He will give you more responsibility and reward.

But the best is this: when your work on earth is
done, you will share eternal life and happiness with
God. ■

An Invitation From the Commander

Military services stress good communication from top to bottom. Commanders want to ensure that all subordinates get all of the information necessary as it pertains to their work and overall welfare. One longtime tradition is the commander's Open Door Policy. It's a standing invitation to meet with the commander.

A typical open door policy might contain something like the following:

I am accessible, at any time, to every member of this unit to assist with any problem or complaint they cannot solve themselves. If a Warrior wants to meet with me, he/she will schedule an appointment through their Chain of Command. Although I encourage it, the Warrior does not have to inform anyone of the reason why he/she wants to talk to me.

This policy will remain in effect until rescinded.

Our Heavenly Commander also has an open door policy. It's a standing invitation to meet with Him to discuss anything, but most importantly, your relationship with Him. Even better is the fact you don't have to get permission from anyone to meet with your Heavenly Commander. You go straight to Him in prayer.

He desires a personal relationship with you. That relationship has been made possible through the work and sacrifice of His Son, Jesus Christ. The biblical term for entering into this relationship with God the Father through Jesus Christ is called salvation. Salvation begins at the time you accept Christ as your Savior and extends throughout eternity. It is the most important decision you can ever make.

Salvation is not something God will force on any person. You must decide.

If you want to take the Commander up on His invitation for salvation, you can do so right now. His Open Door Policy is still in effect. The process is quite simple. To know God and be ready for heaven, follow these steps:

1. Admit you are a sinner. Ask God's forgiveness, and repent of your sins.

There is no one righteous, not even one; . . . for all have sinned and fall short of the glory of God. Romans 3:10,23 (See Romans 5:8; 6:23.)

Everyone who calls on the name of the Lord will be saved. Romans 10:13 (See Acts 3:19.)

Continued on next page

2. Believe in Jesus (put your trust in Him) as your only hope of salvation.

For God so loved the world that he gave his one and only Son, that whoever believes in him shall not perish but have eternal life. John 3:16 (See John 14:6.)

Become a child of God by receiving Christ.

To all who received him, to those who believed in his name, he gave the right to become children of God. John 1:12 (See Revelation 3:20.)

3. Confess that Jesus is your Lord.

If you declare with your mouth, "Jesus is Lord," and believe in your heart that God raised him from the dead, you will be saved. Romans 10:9 (See verse 10.)

If you would like someone to pray with you concerning your decision to follow Jesus Christ, please contact a military chaplain or local pastor.

Following your decision to follow Christ, we strongly recommend becoming involved in a local chapel or church. People there will help you in your Christian growth and development.

A few last words. Although multiplied millions have made decisions to follow Christ, each situation is personal and unique. Some people experience a high level of emotion. Others make a firm, but quiet choice to follow the Master.

Each person's experience is unique and different, but all come to salvation through faith. There is no other way. We don't deserve it. We can't earn it or buy it. We simply receive it by faith.

For it is by grace you have been saved, through
faith — and this not from yourselves,
it is the gift of God.
(Ephesians 2:8)

If you have not yet made a decision to follow Christ, won't you make that decision today? Tomorrow is not promised. Today is the day of salvation. ■

Life can be extremely difficult, but God's Word has the help we need to navigate through life's storms.

God never promised a carefree life when we accept Christ as our Lord and Savior. In fact, Scripture is replete with the truth that we will have troubles in this life. However, the Bible also assures us that these trials have a purpose and that God can give us victory in the middle of overwhelming challenges.

As we cry out to God for help, He can turn difficulty into our personal tutor that will reveal more fully the love He has for us and His plan for our lives. Whether it is an attack from the devil, a trial handpicked by God to grow us in a particular area, or a hardship we cause ourselves, God knows how to give us hope in the middle of trials. He will deliver us through adversity, and grow our faith in Him.

We pray that the following Scriptures will give you hope, truth, and perspective that will help you as you navigate through the hardest trials of your life.

The Scriptures are listed in biblical order, from Genesis to Revelation. We encourage you to look them up in the Bible for yourself and read them in context. (All Scripture quotations are from the New International Version.)

Deuteronomy 8:5

Know then in your heart that as a man disciplines his son, so the LORD your God disciplines you.

Job 23:10
But he knows the way that I take; when he has tested me, I will come forth as gold.

Psalm 50:15
Call upon me in the day of trouble; I will deliver you, and you will honor me.

Psalm 66:8–14
[8] Praise our God, all peoples, let the sound of his praise be heard;

[9] he has preserved our lives and kept our feet from slipping.

[10] For you, God, tested us; you refined us like silver.

[11] You brought us into prison and laid burdens on our backs.

[12] You let people ride over our heads; we went through fire and water, but you brought us to a place of abundance.

[13] I will come to your temple with burnt offerings and fulfill my vows to you —

[14] vows my lips promised and my mouth spoke when I was in trouble.

Psalm 86:7
When I am in distress, I call to you, because you answer me.

Psalm 107:6
Then they cried out to the LORD in their trouble, and he delivered them from their distress.

Psalm 119:67
Before I was afflicted I went astray, but now I obey your word.

Psalm 119:75–77
[75] I know, LORD, that your laws are righteous, and that in faithfulness you have afflicted me.
[76] May your unfailing love be my comfort, according to your promise to your servant.
[77] Let your compassion come to me that I may live, for your law is my delight.

Psalm 124:1–4
[1] If the LORD had not been on our side — let Israel say —
[2] if the LORD had not been on our side when people attacked us,
[3] they would have swallowed us alive, when their anger flared against us;
[4] the flood would have engulfed us, the torrent would have swept over us.

Psalm 138:7
Though I walk in the midst of trouble, you preserve my life. You stretch out your hand against the anger of my foes, with your right hand you save me.

Proverbs 3:11–12

¹¹ My son, do not despise the LORD's discipline, and do not resent his rebuke, ¹² because the LORD disciplines those he loves, as a father the son he delights in.

Matthew 5:10–12

¹⁰ Blessed are those who are persecuted because of righteousness, for theirs is the kingdom of heaven. ¹¹ Blessed are you when people insult you, persecute you and falsely say all kinds of evil against you because of me. ¹² Rejoice and be glad, because great is your reward in heaven, for in the same way they persecuted the prophets who were before you.

Mark 4:16–17

¹⁶ Others, like seed sown on rocky places, hear the word and at once receive it with joy. ¹⁷ But since they have no root, they last only a short time. When trouble or persecution comes because of the word, they quickly fall away.

Luke 4:1–2

¹ Jesus, full of the Holy Spirit, left the Jordan and was led by the Spirit into the wilderness, ² where for forty days he was tempted by the devil. He ate nothing during those days, and at the end of them he was hungry.

John 15:18–20

¹⁸ "If the world hates you, keep in mind that it hated me first. ¹⁹ If you belonged to the world, it would love you

as its own. As it is, you do not belong to the world, but I have chosen you out of the world. That is why the world hates you. [20]Remember what I told you: 'A servant is not greater than his master.' If they persecuted me, they will persecute you also. If they obeyed my teaching, they will obey yours also."

John 16:1–4

[1]"All this I have told you so that you will not fall away. [2]They will put you out of the synagogue; in fact, the time is coming when anyone who kills you will think they are offering a service to God. [3]They will do such things because they have not known the Father or me. [4]I have told you this, so that when the time comes you will remember that I warned you about them. I did not tell you this at first because I was with you."

John 16:33

I have told you these things, so that in me you may have peace. In this world you will have trouble. But take heart! I have overcome the world.

Acts 5:40–41

[40]His speech persuaded them. They called the apostles in and had them flogged. Then they ordered them not to speak in the name of Jesus, and let them go. [41]The apostles left the Sanhedrin, rejoicing because they had been counted worthy of suffering disgrace for the Name.

Romans 5:3–5

³ Not only so, but we also glory in our sufferings, because we know that suffering produces perseverance; ⁴ perseverance, character; and character, hope. ⁵ And hope does not put us to shame, because God's love has been poured out into our hearts through the Holy Spirit, who has been given to us.

Romans 8:17–18

¹⁷ Now if we are children, then we are heirs — heirs of God and coheirs with Christ, if indeed we share in his sufferings in order that we may also share in his glory. ¹⁸ I consider that our present sufferings are not worth comparing with the glory that will be revealed in us.

Romans 8:35

Who shall separate us from the love of Christ? Shall trouble or hardship or persecution or famine or nakedness or danger or sword?

Romans 15:4–5

⁴ For everything that was written in the past was written to teach us, so that through the endurance taught in the Scriptures and the encouragement they provide we might have hope. ⁵ May the God who gives endurance and encouragement give you the same attitude of mind toward each other that Christ Jesus had.

1 Corinthians 10:13
No temptation has overtaken you except what is common to mankind. And God is faithful; he will not let you be tempted beyond what you can bear. But when you are tempted, he will also provide a way out so that you can endure it.

2 Corinthians 1:3–5
³Praise be to the God and Father of our Lord Jesus Christ, the Father of compassion and the God of all comfort, ⁴who comforts us in all our troubles, so that we can comfort those in any trouble with the comfort we ourselves receive from God. ⁵For just as we share abundantly in the sufferings of Christ, so also our comfort abounds through Christ

2 Corinthians 4:8–10
⁸We are hard pressed on every side, but not crushed; perplexed, but not in despair; ⁹persecuted, but not abandoned; struck down, but not destroyed. ¹⁰We always carry around in our body the death of Jesus, so that the life of Jesus may also be revealed in our body.

2 Corinthians 7:5–7
⁵For when we came into Macedonia, we had no rest, but we were harassed at every turn — conflicts on the outside, fears within. ⁶But God, who comforts the downcast, comforted us by the coming of Titus, ⁷and not only by his coming but also by the comfort you had given him. He told us about your longing for me,

your deep sorrow, your ardent concern for me, so that my joy was greater than ever.

2 Corinthians 12:9–10

[9] But he said to me, "My grace is sufficient for you, for my power is made perfect in weakness." Therefore I will boast all the more gladly about my weaknesses, so that Christ's power may rest on me. [10] That is why, for Christ's sake, I delight in weaknesses, in insults, in hardships, in persecutions, in difficulties. For when I am weak, then I am strong.

Philippians 1:29–30

[29] For it has been granted to you on behalf of Christ not only to believe in him, but also to suffer for him, [30] since you are going through the same struggle you saw I had, and now hear that I still have.

2 Timothy 2:3

Join with me in suffering, like a good soldier of Christ Jesus.

Hebrews 2:18

Because he himself suffered when he was tempted, he is able to help those who are being tempted.

Hebrews 5:7–8

[7] During the days of Jesus' life on earth, he offered up prayers and petitions with fervent cries and tears to the

one who could save him from death, and he was heard because of his reverent submission. [8] Son though he was, he learned obedience from what he suffered.

Hebrews 10:32–34

[32] Remember those earlier days after you had received the light, when you endured in a great conflict full of suffering. [33] Sometimes you were publicly exposed to insult and persecution; at other times you stood side by side with those who were so treated. [34] You suffered along with those in prison and joyfully accepted the confiscation of your property, because you knew that you yourselves had better and lasting possessions.

Hebrews 12:1–3

[1] Let us throw off everything that hinders and the sin that so easily entangles. And let us run with perseverance the race marked out for us, [2] fixing our eyes on Jesus, the pioneer and perfecter of faith. For the joy set before him he endured the cross, scorning its shame, and sat down at the right hand of the throne of God. [3] Consider him who endured such opposition from sinners, so that you will not grow weary and lose heart.

Hebrews 12:5–6

[5] And have you completely forgotten this word of encouragement that addresses you as a father addresses

his son? It says, "My son, do not make light of the Lord's discipline, and do not lose heart when he rebukes you, [6] because the Lord disciplines the one he loves, and he chastens everyone he accepts as his son."

Hebrews 12:7–8

[7] Endure hardship as discipline; God is treating you as his children. For what child is not disciplined by their father? [8] If you are not disciplined — and everyone undergoes discipline — then you are not legitimate, not true sons and daughters at all.

James 1:2–4

[2] Consider it pure joy, my brothers,and sisters, whenever you face trials of many kinds, [3] because you know that the testing of your faith produces perseverance. [4] Let perseverance finish its work so that you may be mature and complete, not lacking anything.

James 1:12

Blessed is the one who perseveres under trial because, having stood the test, that person will receive the crown of life that the Lord has promised to those who love him.

James 5:13

Is anyone among you in trouble? Let them pray. Is anyone happy? Let them sing songs of praise.

1 Peter 1:6–7

⁶In this you greatly rejoice, though now for a little while you may have had to suffer grief in all kinds of trials. ⁷These have come so that the proven genuineness of your faith — of greater worth than gold, which perishes even though refined by fire — may result in praise, glory and honor when Jesus Christ is revealed.

1 Peter 2:19–21

¹⁹For it is commendable if someone bears up under the pain of unjust suffering because he is conscious of God. ²⁰But how is it to your credit if you receive a beating for doing wrong and endure it? But if you suffer for doing good and you endure it, this is commendable before God. ²¹To this you were called, because Christ suffered for you, leaving you an example, that you should follow in his steps.

1 Peter 4:1–2

¹Therefore, since Christ suffered in his body, arm yourselves also with the same attitude, because whoever suffers in the body is done with sin. ²As a result, they do not live the rest of their earthly lives for evil human desires, but rather for the will of God.

1 Peter 4:12–13

¹²Dear friends, do not be surprised at the fiery ordeal that has come on you to test you, as though something strange were happening to you. ¹³But rejoice inasmuch

as you participate in the sufferings of Christ, so that you may be overjoyed when his glory is revealed.

1 Peter 5:9–11

[9]Resist him [the devil], standing firm in the faith, because you know that your brothers throughout the world are undergoing the same kind of sufferings. [10]And the God of all grace, who called you to his eternal glory in Christ, after you have suffered a little while, will himself restore you and make you strong, firm and steadfast. [11] to him be the power for ever and ever. Amen.

2 Peter 2:9

If this is so, then the Lord knows how to rescue the godly from trials and to hold the unrighteous for punishment on the day of judgment.

Revelation 2:10

Do not be afraid of what you are about to suffer. I tell you, the devil will put some of you in prison to test you, and you will suffer persecution for ten days. Be faithful, even to the point of death, and I will give you life as your victor's crown.

Scott and Judy McChrystal

Chaplain (Colonel) Scott McChrystal, United States Army Retired, served 31 years on active duty, 10 as an infantry officer and the remainder as an Army chaplain. His line officer experience included a tour in Vietnam as an Infantry Platoon Leader and three assignments with the 82nd Airborne Division at Fort Bragg, North Carolina. As an Army chaplain, he had multiple tours at home and abroad. His final assignment was as the senior chaplain at the United States Military Academy at West Point, New York.

Judy and Scott have been married 38 years. Judy has taught math in junior high and high school, and in Christian schools in many places they have been stationed. She kept the home fires burning and the four children on schedule when Scott was gone. She has worked alongside Scott in ministry for 30 years. She is a gifted Bible teacher and counselor. For the past 6 years, she has been a teacher and mentor to women whose husbands are preparing for ministry as military chaplains.

Scott presently serves as the Military/VA Representative and Endorser within the Chaplaincy Department for The General Council of the Assemblies of God. Scott and Judy live in Springfield, Missouri, and have 4 children and 7 grandchildren. ∎

Above, Chaplain McChrystal prepares to deliver a public prayer at the United States Military Academy at West Point, New York, 2003.

Judy and Scott McChrystal

The Old Testament speaks about a man who lived almost four thousand years ago. His name was Job, and during his time of earth, he experienced some incredibly horrific storms, yet managed to survive them and live a long, prosperous life. In the midst of his suffering and travail, he wrote these words:

> *Man born of woman is of few days*
> *and full of trouble.*
> *(Job 14:1)*

And yet if we read to the end of the Book of Job, we find that his outlook and understanding of God had matured greatly. Job learned that God's thoughts were higher than his and God's ways were much higher than his own. He apologized to God as reflected in these words:

> *My ears had heard of you but now my eyes have*
> *seen you. Therefore I despise myself and*
> *repent in dust and ashes.*
> *(Job 42:5–6)*

Job got it right when he said that man's days are full of trouble. But like Job, we can learn that life's storms are not all bad. In fact, the Lord uses them to teach us many things and to help us grow in our faith.

We trust that the material in *Navigating Life's Storms* has been a blessing to you and that you have grown in your knowledge of our awesome God. As future storms occur in your life — and they will — we pray that you will turn to God and His Word for the hope, strength, guidance, and wisdom you'll need as you serve Him. We have every confidence that you will.

We plan to continue our Daily Strength for the Battle series and thank the Lord for assigning us the mission of writing these devotionals. We thank Him also for His favor in allowing us to distribute these volumes to thousands of warriors and their families stationed around the world.

Please check our Web site for information about future volumes. ■

Additional copies of this volume,
as well as other volumes, are available at
Our Web site: www.dailystrengthforthebattle.com
By e-mail: dailystrengthforthebattle@gmail.com
By mail: Warrior Spirit Publications
P.O. Box 8125, Springfield, MO 65801